SCOTLAND'S NEW WRITING THEATRE

Traverse Theatre Company

Petrol Jesus Nightmare #5 (In the Time of the Messiah)

by Henry Adam

cast in order of appearance

Slomo	James Cunningham
Buddy	Aleksandar Mikic
the Texan	Lewis Howden
Yossariat	Joseph Thompson
the Rabbi's Wife	Susan Vidler

Director	Philip Howard
Designer	Soutra Gilmour
Lighting Designer	Charles Balfour
Sound Designer	Graham Sutherland
Fight Director	Terry King
Dialect Coach	Jo Cameron Brown
Assistant Director	Fergus Ford
Stage Manager	Gemma Smith
Deputy Stage Manager	Natasha Lee-Walsh
Assistant Stage Manager	Sarah Holland
Wardrobe Supervisor	Aileen Sherry

First performed at the Traverse Theatre, Friday 28 July 2006

a Traverse Theatre Commission

TRAVERSE THEATRE

Artistic Director Philip Howard

Powerhouse of new writing. (Daily Telegraph)

The Traverse's commissioning process embraces a spirit of innovation and risk-taking that has launched the careers of many of Scotland's best-known writers including John Byrne, David Greig and David Harrower. It is unique in Scotland in that it fulfils the crucial role of providing the infrastructure, professional support and expertise to ensure the development of a dynamic theatre culture for Scotland.

The importance of the Traverse is difficult to overestimate . . . without the theatre, it is difficult to imagine Scottish playwriting at all. (Sunday Times)

From its conception in the 1960s, the Traverse has remained a pivotal venue during the Edinburgh Festival. It receives enormous critical and audience acclaim for its programming, as well as regularly winning awards. In 2001, the hugely successful *Gagarin Way* by Gregory Burke won Fringe First and Herald Angel Awards. This was also the year the Traverse received a Herald Archangel Award for overall artistic excellence. In 2002, the Traverse produced award-winning shows, *Outlying Islands* by David Greig and *Iron* by Rona Munro and in 2003, *The People Next Door* by Henry Adam won Fringe First and Herald Angel Awards. In 2004, the Traverse produced the award-winning *Shimmer* by Linda McLean and a stage adaptation by David Greig of Raja Shehadeh's diary account of the Israeli occupation of Ramallah, *When the Bulbul Stopped Singing.* The Traverse's 2005 programme received a record total of 12 awards, including a Fringe First for its own production, *East Coast Chicken Supper* by Martin J Taylor.

One of Europe's most important homes for new plays. (Sunday Herald)

The Traverse's success isn't limited to either the Edinburgh stage or the Festival. Since 2001, *Gagarin Way, Outlying Islands, Iron, The People Next Door, When the Bulbul Stopped Singing,* the *Slab Boys Trilogy, Mr Placebo* and *Helmet* have toured not only within Scotland and the UK, but in Sweden, Norway, the Balkans, Germany, USA, Iran and Canada.

Auld Reekie's most important theatre. (The Times)

Now in its 14th year, the Traverse's annual Highlands & Islands tour is a crucial strand of our work. This commitment to Scottish touring has taken plays from our Edinburgh home to audiences all over Scotland. The Traverse has criss-crossed the nation performing at diverse locations from Shetland to Dumfries, Aberdeen to Benbecula. The Traverse's 2005 production *I was a Beautiful Day* was commissioned to open the new An Lanntair Arts Centre in Stornoway, Isle of Lewis.

The Traverse Theatre has established itself as Scotland's leading exponent of new writing, with a reputation that extends worldwide. (The Scotsman)

The Traverse's work with young people is of supreme importance and takes the form of encouraging playwriting through its flagship education project *Class Act*, as well as the Young Writers' Groups. *Class Act* is now in its 16th year and gives pupils the opportunity to develop their plays with professional playwrights and work with directors and actors to see the finished piece performed on stage at the Traverse. This year, for the third year running, the project also took place in Russia. In 2004 *Articulate*, a large scale project based on the *Class Act* model, took place in West Dunbartonshire working with 11 to 14 year olds. The hugely successful Young Writers' Groups are open to new writers aged between 16 and 25.

The Traverse has an unrivalled reputation for producing contemporary theatre of the highest quality, invention and energy, and for its dedication to new writing. (Scotland on Sunday)

The Traverse is committed to working with international playwrights and, in 2005, produced *In the Bag* by Wang Xiaoli in a version by Ronan O'Donnell, the first-ever full production of a contemporary Chinese play in the UK. This project was part of the successful Playwrights in Partnership scheme, which unites international and Scottish writers, and brings the most dynamic new global voices to the Edinburgh stage. Other international Traverse partnerships have included work from Québec, Norway, France, Finland, Italy, Portugal, Belgium and Japan.

www.traverse.co.uk

To find out about ways in which you can support the work of the Traverse please contact Ruth Allan or Vikki Graves 0131 228 3223 or development@traverse.co.uk

Charity No. SC002368

COMPANY BIOGRAPHIES

Henry Adam (Writer)

Henry was born in Wick, Caithness. His last Traverse Theatre production, *The People Next Door*, won Fringe First and Herald Angel awards at the 2003 Edinburgh Fringe Festival. It has toured Scotland, England, Germany, the Balkans and New York. Also for the Traverse: *Among Unbroken Hearts* (Traverse/The Bush Theatre; Meyer Whitworth Award Winner 2002), *The Widow* (as part of Sharp Shorts). Other plays include *When the Dons were Kings* (The Lemon Tree); *An Clo Mor* (Theatre Highland); *Millennium - Angels of Paris* (His Majesty's, Aberdeen); *The Abattoir* (The Lemon Tree; Mobil Scottish Playwriting Competition Winner).

Charles Balfour (Lighting Designer)

Charles has worked extensively in dance, theatre and opera. Theatre credits include *Cleansed* (Oxford Stage Company); *The Tempest* (Liverpool Playhouse); *Hair, Woyzeck, Witness, The Gentleman from Olmedo, Turn of the Screw* (The Gate); *Therese Raquin, Baby Doll, Bash* (Citizens Theatre); *Master Class* (Derby Playhouse); *Hedda Gabler* (West Yorkshire Playhouse); *Grace* (Birmingham Rep). His work for dance includes Stuttgart Ballet, Richard Alston, Birmingham Royal Ballet, Aletta Collins, Matthew Hawkins and David Massingam. His work for opera includes Opera North, London Sinfonietta and Alderburgh Festival.

Jo Cameron Brown (Dialect Coach)

Jo trained at the Central School of Drama and RSAMD. She has worked as a dialect coach in theatre, television and film. Theatre credits include *Whistle Down the Wind, Footloose, Smoking with Lulu* (West End). Television credits include *Losing Gemma, The Kindness of Strangers, Island at War* (ITV); *Low Winter Sun* (Tiger Aspect/Channel 4); *Sweeney Todd* (Box TV/Size 9/BBC); *Anchor Me* (Granada). Film credits include *Brick Lane* (Anapurna Films); *Hallam Foe* (FilmFour/Lunar Films/Scottish Screen); *The Restraint of Beasts* (Apocalypso Pictures); *Nina's Heavenly Delights* (Priority Pictures); *An American Haunting* (Midsummer Films); *Luminal* (Dreyco Productions); *Dear Frankie* (Scorpio Films Ltd); *Young Adam* (Recorded Picture Company); *The I Inside* (Miramax Films); *The Extremists* (The Carousel Picture Company S.A.); *28 Days Later* (DNA Films). Jo has also worked extensively as an actress in theatre and television. Her theatre credits include *Perfect Days* (Traverse); *Square Rounds, Guys and Dolls* (National Theatre). Her television credits include *Judge John Deed, River City, The Singing Detective, Great Expectations* (BBC).

James Cunningham (*Slomo*)
James trained at the Welsh College of Music and Drama. For the
Traverse: *One Day All This Will Come to Nothing, Green Field,
Abandonment*. Other theatre credits include *The Wonderful World of
Dissocia* (EIF/Theatre Royal, Plymouth/Tron Theatre); *Passing Places*
(Derby Playhouse/Greenwich Theatre); *Cleansed, Penetrator* (Royal
Court); *You'll Have Had Your Hole* (London Astoria II); *Marabou Stork
Nightmares* (Citizens Theatre/Leicester Haymarket Theatre);
Trainspotting (Citizens Theatre). Television credits include *Murphy's
Law* (Tiger Aspect); *Rebus, Taggart* (SMG); *Rockface* (BBC); *Bumping
the Odds* (Wall To Wall). Film credits include *Sixteen Years of Alcohol*
(Tartan Works Ltd); *American Cousins* (Bard Entertainments Ltd);
Snatch (SKA Films); *War Requiem* (BBC Films).

Soutra Gilmour (Designer)
Soutra trained at the Wimbledon School of Art. Theatre credits
include *A Brief History of Helen of Troy* (ATC); *Hair, Electra, The Flu
Season* (The Gate); *Baby Doll, Therese Raquin, Antigone* (Citizens
Theatre); *Country Music* (Royal Court); *Mr Nobody, Animal* (Soho
Theatre); *The Snow Queen* (Dundee Rep). Her work for opera includes
Saul, Hansel & Gretel (Opera North); *Cosi Fan Tutte, Mary Queen of
Scots* (English Touring Opera); *Trouble in Tahiti, Mahagonny Sonspeil,
Walking Not Driving* (The Opera Group); *Bake for One Hour,
Corridors, A Better Place* (ENO). Work for film, as Costume Designer,
includes *The Follower* (Northern Ireland Film Commission); *Amazing
Grace* (Parallax Pictures).

Philip Howard (Director)
Philip trained under Max Stafford-Clark at the Royal Court Theatre,
London, on the Regional Theatre Young Director Scheme from 1988-
1990. He was Associate Director at the Traverse from 1993-1996,
and has been Artistic Director since 1996. Productions at the Traverse
include 19 world premieres of plays by David Greig, David Harrower,
Catherine Czerkawska, Catherine Grosvenor, Jules Horne, Ronan
O'Donnell, Nicola McCartney, Linda McLean, Sue Glover, Iain Heggie,
Iain F MacLeod and the late Iain Crichton Smith. Fringe First awards
for *Kill the Old Torture Their Young, Wiping My Mother's Arse* and
Outlying Islands. Other productions at the Traverse include *Faith Healer*
by Brian Friel, *The Trestle at Pope Lick Creek* by Naomi Wallace,
Cuttin' a Rug by John Byrne, *When the Bulbul Stopped Singing* by Raja
Shehadeh (also Fadjr International Festival, Tehran; Off-Broadway,
New York) and, as Co-Director, *Solemn Mass for a Full Moon in
Summer* by Michel Tremblay (Traverse/Barbican). Productions elsewhere
include *Words of Advice for Young People* by Ioanna Anderson

(Rough Magic, Dublin), *The Speculator* by David Greig in Catalan (Grec Festival, Barcelona/Edinburgh International Festival), *Entertaining Mr Sloane* (Royal, Northampton) and *Something About Us* (Lyric Hammersmith Studio). Radio credits include *The Gold Digger* by Iain F MacLeod, *Being Norwegian* by David Greig (BBC Radio Scotland); *The Room* by Paul Brennan (BBC Radio 4).

Lewis Howden (*the Texan*)

Lewis trained at the RSAMD. For the Traverse: *The Nest, Olga, Knives in Hens, Loose Ends, The House Among the Stars*. Other theatre credits include *Tartuffe, Merlin the Magnificent, Mother Courage, Cuttin' a Rug, Changed Days*, (Royal Lyceum, Edinburgh); *No Mean City, Nightingale and Chase* (Citizens Theatre*); Macbeth, Medea, King Lear* (Theatre Babel); *Frankie and Johnny* (Rapture Theatre); *Beauty Queen of Leenanne, The Trick is to Keep Breathing* (Tron Theatre); *Riddance* (Paines Plough); *Caged Heat, The Big Funk, The Crucible, Glengarry Glen Ross* (The Arches); *Fire in the Basement* (Communicado); *The Angel's Share* (Borderline); *Quelques Fleurs* (Nippy Sweeties); *On the Sidelines* (Oran Mor); *Electra* (Diva Theatre Company). Television credits include *Taggart, Rebus, Dr Finlay, The Chief, Butterfingers* (STV); *Monarch of the Glen, Strathblair, The Conegatherers, Robert Louis Stevenson* (BBC); *Turning World* (Channel 4). Radio credits include *Offside in Bohemia, Mapping the Heart, Rebus, An Island Between Heaven and Earth, Playing a Blinder, An Ember in the Straw, Always on my Mind, Cuba, The Blasphemer, Poetry Please* (BBC). Film credits include *Aberdeen* (Freeway Films); *The Blue Boy* (BBC); *Gare Au Male* (Animula); *Slide* (Top Left Productions).

Fergus Ford (Assistant Director)

Fergus trained at QMUC and graduated in 2006. As Assistant Director, theatre credits include *Faust Parts One & Two* (Royal Lyceum, Edinburgh); *The World* (The Byre/QMUC). Directing credits, whilst training, include *The Fire Raisers, Comedy Shorts* (QMUC); *My Morocco, Hypocrite* (Rapid Theatre); *Much ado about Cutlery, The Ring of Power* (Battered Hat Productions); *Carnival Bone* (RLD Theatre Co.). As Co-Director, theatre credits include *Arturo Ui, Welcome to the Moon* (Life After 90).

Terry King (Fight Director)

For the Traverse: *East Coast Chicken Supper, The People Next Door, Iron, Gagarin Way*. Other theatre credits include *Fool For Love, King Lear, Othello, Henry V, London Cuckolds, Ting Tang Mine, The Duchess of Malfi, Jerry Springer – The Opera, Elmina's Kitchen, Edmond* (National Theatre); *Troilus and Cressida, Romeo and Juliet,*

Cymbeline, Pericles, Twelfth Night, Henry IV Pts 1 & 2, Henry VI Pts 1, 2 & 3, Macbeth, The Jacobean Season, Coriolanus (RSC); *The Recruiting Officer, Search and Destroy, Ashes and Sand, Oleanna, Berlin Bertie, Greenland* (Royal Court); *Festen* (Lyric, Shaftesbury Avenue); *Caligula, Accidental Death of an Anarchist* (Donmar Warehouse); *Lysistrata* (The Old Vic); *Death of a Salesman* (Bristol Old Vic); *Of Mice and Men* (Nottingham Playhouse). He has also worked extensively in opera, musicals and television.

Aleksandar Mikic (*Buddy*)
Aleksandar trained at RSAMD, the National Theatre of Bosnia and Herzegovina and The Drama Studio of Tuzla, Bosnia. Theatre credits include *5/11, King Lear, The Government Inspector* (Chichester Festival Theatre); *Cruel & Tender* (Young Vic); *Gilt* (7:84); *Britannicus, The Cherry Orchard, Suddenly Last Summer* (Citizens Theatre). Television credits include *Blue Murder, The Last Detective* (Granada TV); *Comic Strip Presents: Pampas Grass* (Great Western Features); *Footballers' Wives* (Shed Productions); *Holby City, Face at the Window, Auf Wiedersehen Pet* (BBC); *Prime Suspect* (LWT); *Ultimate Force* (Bentley Productions/ITV); *Messiah* (BBC Northern Ireland/Paramount/Vengeance); *Spooks* (Kudos). Film credits include *Rendition* (Ultrafilms); *Mine* (Kaos Films); *The Ticking Man* (Roaring Fire Film); *Black Olive, London Kebabs* (NFST).

Graham Sutherland (Sound Designer)
Graham trained at Glasgow University. For the Traverse: *Outlying Islands* (Scottish Tour: Relights). Graham has worked extensively in theatre as a Lighting Designer, Sound Designer and Technical Stage Manager. As Sound Designer, theatre credits include *Slope, Blingsight* (Untitled Projects); *Freefall* (7:84); *Stacy* (Hush Productions); *Snuff* (The Arches). As Lighting Designer, theatre credits include *Good Sister Bad, Fergus Steps Out* (Lung Ha's Theatre Company); *Home - Dundee* (NTS); *Snuff* (The Arches); *Voyager Princess* (Sense Scotland); *Dying For It* (SYT); *Seeing Voices* (Solar Bear). As Technical Stage Manger, theatre credits include *Dead End* (Toonspeak) and work for the Bank of Scotland Children's International Theatre Festival. Until recently, Graham was based at the Citizens Theatre where he was Associate Lighting Designer on *Blood Wedding* and *Romeo and Juliet* but now works as a freelance Sound and Lighting Designer.

Joseph Thompson (*Yossarian*)
Joseph trained at the Webber Douglas Academy of Dramatic Art, graduating in 2005. Theatre credits include *The Voysey Inheritance* (National Theatre); *Romeo and Juliet* (Royal Exchange Theatre);

Undertow (Bristol Old Vic Studio); *Lessness* (Drama Festival, Amsterdam). Television credits include *Trafalgar ER* (JH Films); *Invitation to a Hanging* (Channel 4/Juniper).

Susan Vidler (*the Rabbi's Wife*)

Susan trained at the Welsh College of Music and Drama. For the Traverse: *The Juju Girl*. Other theatre credits include *A Thousand Yards* (Southwark Playhouse); *Sabina, Trainspotting, The Present* (The Bush Theatre); *Trainspotting* (Citizens Theatre/Traverse); *Heartless* (ICA, London); *A Better Day* (Theatre Royal Stratford East). Television credits include *England Expects, The Woman in White, Macbeth on the Estate, Stone Cold, Flowers of the Forest, Dark Adapted Eye, Casualty* (BBC); *The Last Detective, Cracker* (Granada TV); *Terry McIntyre* (BBC Scotland); *The Jump* (Warner Sister); *Impact* (Company Television); *Love In The Twenty First Century* (Red Productions); *Kavanagh QC* (Carlton TV). Film credits include *Voices From Afar, Poppies* (Troicka Ltd); *Wilbur Wants To Kill Himself* (Zentropa Productions); *Trainspotting* (Figment Films/Channel 4); *Naked* (Thin Man Films); *Alone* (CFI Ltd); *The Present* (Fenix/Playground); *The Passport* (B&L Media); *California Sunshine* (Sigma Film/Channel 4); *That Old One* (Ideal World Productions); *Memory Man* (RDF Television); *Clueless* (Curious Pictures).

SPONSORSHIP AND DEVELOPMENT

We would like to thank the following
corporate sponsors for their support

To find out more, please contact
Ruth Allan or Vikki Graves
0131 228 3223 or development@traverse.co.uk

The Traverse Theatre's work
would not be possible without the support of

ARE YOU DEVOTED?

TRAVERSE THEATRE - THE COMPANY

PETROL JESUS NIGHTMARE #5
(IN THE TIME OF THE MESSIAH)

Henry Adam

'What a thick dark cloud that is!' she said.
'And how fast it comes.'

Lewis Carroll, *Through the Looking Glass*

Characters

SLOMO

BUDDY

TEXAN

YOSSARIAT

RABBI'S WIFE

This text went to press before the end of rehearsals so may differ slightly from the play as performed.

ONE

Sound of a tinkling Viennese piano. A tour guide-cum-circus barker marshals a crowd of tourists, pointing out the places of antiquity in Jerusalem's old town. Panic.

Some poor guy's living room. A flat block in occupied territory. The rat-runs inside and beneath.

Visible graffiti: FUCK YOU YOU MURDERING MOTHERFUCKING WORLD BANK WHORES, ERZET YISRAEL, IDF=NWO.

Crucifixes of light pierce the air through the stencilled shutters covering the only window. In the half-light, little is visible. A young soldier, SLOMO, approaches the window, unhooking the shutters with his rifle barrel. Another soldier, BUDDY, sits against the wall near a hole in the connecting wall, breathing heavily. This hole is like a mouse-hole but large enough for a man to pass through – partially covered by a board that has until recently been nailed over the hole. The hole is for ease of access for men in uniform. The board is for the convenience and privacy of the occupant – an effort at normality.

Belongings, half scattered, half in their proper place, become visible, much of which are Western, much iconic and kitsch – the detritus of dreams. SLOMO controls the light in the room as he checks the view for signs of danger and opportunity. He speaks to BUDDY or to the air as he does, shrugging often, as if unsure of his own history.

SLOMO. My mother died when I was four. Did I tell you?

BUDDY's hands hold a book – a Bible – that he has picked from the floor. His eyes stare straight ahead. BUDDY's fear is just beneath the surface, affecting him like too much caffeine. SLOMO's fear is buried deeper, and is more permanent. His lack of understanding protects him and makes him susceptible to boredom. He needs constant distraction, even in a war zone.

Sporadic gunfire punctuates the action.

Not much.

Not much. Time.

Four years.

CAPTAIN YOSSARIAT *looks up from the tattered Israeli flag in his hands. The* RABBI'S WIFE's *haute couture seems incongruous in a war zone.*

Lot of love I think.

I mean.

Buddy?

BUDDY. I'm listening.

SLOMO. How do you remember?

How do you not forget?

Sporadic gunfire is heard in the distance. YOSSARIAT *gets to his feet, dropping the flag at his feet.*

The RABBI'S WIFE *laughs at* YOSSARIAT *and his flag.*

My father took it bad.

Didn't speak her name.

I needed him to speak.

To say her name.

I needed him to. Keep her.

Keep her safe.

Until I was.

You know?

Until I could.

He burned all her pictures.

Her clothes.

I found some though.

Under his bed.

Pictures.

He beat me.

Beat me when he found they were.

Who else would. I mean.

But I knew.

Knew if I told him he'd burn them too.

And they were all.

All I had.

This is her.

Look.

SLOMO *produces a pornographic magazine from his jacket, open at a certain set of pictures. He pushes the magazine towards* BUDDY.

You can tell she was a nice person, can't you?

A loving person.

She's got nice eyes.

BUDDY. That's not your mother.

SLOMO. Yes, it's my mother.

BUDDY. It's just some tart in a porn mag.

SLOMO. Look at the name.

BUDDY. What?

SLOMO. Look at the name.

That's my mother's name.

That's my mother.

BUDDY. That was her name?

SLOMO. Yes.

BUDDY. And she looked like that?

SLOMO. Yes.

BUDDY. You remember?

SLOMO *nods vigorously.*

BUDDY *shrugs and hands him the magazine.*

Nice jugs.

SLOMO. Thank you.

That's my mother.

SLOMO *returns to the window.*

My mother thanks you.

BUDDY. Fucking hell.

SLOMO *nods towards the Bible.*

SLOMO. What's that?

BUDDY *holds the Bible up questioningly.*

BUDDY. Bible. Found it lying there.

SLOMO. What's it about?

BUDDY. It's a Bible.

SLOMO. Yeah.

What's it about?

BUDDY *'s look says – Are you serious?* SLOMO *'s look says – Yes.* BUDDY *is at a loss.*

BUDDY. I don't know. Israelites?

SLOMO. Israelites?

BUDDY. Yeah. You know who the Israelites are, don't you?

They taught you that much at school?

SLOMO *giggles.*

Yeah. It's about the Israelites and their divine place in God's plan.

How they wandered around the desert for a couple of thousand years looking for a place to live.

Then when they find one, one of them goes mad. Tells the rest of them he's God.

SLOMO. Was he?

BUDDY *'s body language says – What do you think? Moments pass.*

So what happened to him?

Guy said he was God?

BUDDY *'s look says – You don't know?* SLOMO *shakes his head.*

BUDDY. They built a big cross. Out of wood. And they laid him on it. Like this. See.

BUDDY *spreads his arms, then spreads* SLOMO *'s arms against the wall.* SLOMO *giggles.*

Then they took some nails. And they hammered nails though him.

Through his hands.

His feet.

They hoisted him up.

And left him there.

Blood dripping.

Three days he hung there.

Three days in forty-degree heat.

Freezing nights. Just hanging there.

Any other country they would have put him in a hospital and given him drugs until the voices stopped.

But this was Jerusalem.

They take things like that seriously in Jerusalem.

You never heard that story before?

SLOMO. I don't know.

BUDDY *takes over at the window.*

So. Did he die?

BUDDY. Who?

SLOMO. Guy said he was God.

BUDDY. Like a bitch by all accounts.

SLOMO *settles down with his magazine.*

SLOMO. Should have put him to hospital, eh?

BUDDY. Should've shoved an M-16 up his arse and pulled the fucking trigger.

SLOMO *finds this really funny. His unexpected laughter cheers* BUDDY. *The two men relax together.* BUDDY *nods toward* SLOMO's *magazine.*

That's not your mother, is it?

SLOMO. Nah. Just a magazine.

Thought I'd maybe swap it with somebody.

For chocolate.

Got a sweet tooth.

No kidding.

Sweet tooth and a mum I can't remember.

Five-year contract.

Pair of boots.

Heckler.

Heckler and Koch.

Rabbit's foot.

Mess tin.

Cutlery.

Water bottle.

Three cigarettes.

Pain in my chest when I run.

Trousers.

Calvins.

Vest.

Got some body armour but that's back in the other place.

Other place don't count.

Toothpick.

BUDDY. Slomo? What you doing?

SLOMO. Listing what I got. What I got.

BUDDY. You got a lot.

SLOMO. Yeah, I got a lot. Lot to be thankful for. Too much
sometimes.

BUDDY. So where'd you get the Heckler?

SLOMO. Picked it off the street.

BUDDY. Yeah?

SLOMO. Beside greaseball.

Greaseball was dead.

BUDDY. Some cultures actually think it's obscene to rob from the
dead.

SLOMO *is struck by the rightness of that. And is skewered by it.*

SLOMO. Yes.

Yes.

I do too.

But.

I'll put it back.

BUDDY. See that you do.

SLOMO *goes to remove it from his pack. He likes this gun and doesn't want to give it back. He heads reluctantly for the mouse-hole.* BUDDY *catches sight.*

Slomo!

SLOMO *turns.*

Not now.

SLOMO *returns. A new hope strikes.*

SLOMO. Maybe I can keep it.

Greaseball wasn't.

Dead.

When the Heckler was stolen.

Dead.

After.

Cause he looked at me.

Looked at me picking it up.

Then.

Then he was dead.

SLOMO *nods solemnly.* BUDDY *smirks.*

BUDDY. Did you kill him?

SLOMO. What?

No . . . ?

No . . . ?

Yes.

Yes I did.

9

SLOMO *laughs at his own private joke, which is wondrously funny.* BUDDY *finds his laughter infectious, but stifles it, going back to the window.* BUDDY *takes a bar of chocolate out of his pocket, breaks off a bit and tosses it to* SLOMO. SLOMO *catches it, delighted.*

BUDDY. Some cultures actually think it's obscene to make people dead. You know that?

SLOMO. I do too.

BUDDY. Do you?

SLOMO. Nah.

Like it.

Like the whole rat-a-tat-tat.

It's good, eh? Something to do.

Sometimes when the . . .

You know? When the rat-a-tat-tat's all over I just want to go round everybody.

Tap them on the shoulder.

'Get up, kid! It's over! Get up!'

Ain't that sort of game though, is it?

Out there.

Different sort of game.

BUDDY. So, when did your mind go?

If you don't mind me asking?

SLOMO. I don't mind.

Don't know if it is gone.

Not really.

Could just be hiding.

It's . . .

It's like a thing. Battery.

Really low.

Sometimes I can use it.

Other times . . .

Phht.

Don't get in the way none.

SLOMO *becomes a drill sergeant.*

'You have no mind, little man! I have your mind! The State has
your mind! Where you're going you won't even need no mind!'
'Yes sir! Sergeant sir! Where I'm going I won't need no mind!'

He chuckles. BUDDY *chuckles. The energy drains from*
SLOMO. *His eyes go dead.*

Last year.

Last year outside Belmina.

The word means something to BUDDY. *He is suddenly looking*
at a new phenomenon.

BUDDY. You were at Belmina?

SLOMO *nods, not understanding.*

SLOMO. Uh-huh.

Outside.

Outside Belmina.

BUDDY *touches* SLOMO's *cheek tenderly as he looks in his*
eyes. He smiles as he looks in his eyes. He lightly taps
SLOMO's *cheek with his fingers, twice in rapid succession as*
he looks in his eyes.

BUDDY. Oh, you fucking hero.

BUDDY *turns away.* SLOMO *looks after* BUDDY.

SLOMO. What was that for?

BUDDY. Your Sergeant was right.

Mind can't help you.

No mind. That's where it's at.

You let it all flow over you.

Like it's water in a shower.

Like it's all a fucking dream.

Some bitch religion teaches that.

I forget which one.

SLOMO. Which one?

BUDDY. I don't know! Some bitch!

Does it matter?

I mean, just because some bitch religion says life's a dream, that doesn't make it true, right?

Just like when some bitch says you kill in God's name, you go straight to paradise.

I mean, show me the fucking brochures!

You want me to blow myself up in some street market, I want some fucking guarantees.

Show me the written testimonials!

Show me the fucking photographs!

Show me you're not just full of shit, you fucking full-of-shit bitch!

BUDDY *needs an outlet for his energy. He attacks the walls, the window, punching the shutters open. The open window stuns him for a moment. He runs at it, thrusting his head out the window. He screams violently:*

Allahu Akbar!

An echo comes. Along with gunshots.

Oh, you fucking dogs!

BUDDY *comes inside, trying to calm down. There might be tears in his eyes. He snatches up* SLOMO's *magazine and collapses into a heap.* SLOMO *watches* BUDDY *get his breath back, not quite sure what just went on. He goes to the window and assumes a sniper position.*

SLOMO. I don't want you to blow yourself up in a street market, Buddy.

BUDDY. Good.

SLOMO. You shouldn't get so upset.

I mean . . .

All them gods.

All them gods are pretty much the same.

Aren't they?

BUDDY. Yeah. Pretty much.

SLOMO. Except ours.

> BUDDY *shoots a look at* SLOMO. *Bitterness and disgust cause his head to shake. He tears through the magazine, looking for the one image that will distract him. He rubs his crotch. Which is wet. He throws the magazine aside, disgusted with and preoccupied by the dark patch in his trousers.* SLOMO *continues to watch the street.*

> Did you piss yourself this morning?

> BUDDY *is searching for something.*

BUDDY. I piss myself every morning.

> SLOMO *nods. He too has a stain.*

SLOMO. Never seen so many of them.

> Something made them mad.

BUDDY. Us.

> SLOMO *spins around, as if to say – What did we do? He turns back.*

SLOMO. I'm sick of getting the blame for everything.

BUDDY. Yeah, me too.

> BUDDY *has found a hairdryer and now attempts to dry his crotch. When he switches on the dryer the noise spooks* SLOMO, *who swings round, cocking his rifle.* BUDDY *is milliseconds from death. They exchange eye contact. Both relax at the same time.*

> Fuck.

SLOMO. Sorry.

> BUDDY *freezes, looks at* SLOMO.

> What?

BUDDY. Shat. Shit. Shit!

> BUDDY *smashes the closest thing to him into the floor.* SLOMO *stifles a smile at his indignity.* BUDDY *picks up a cushion lying nearby and rips it apart. He drops his trousers. He pulls the cover off the cushion and tries to wipe the shit off his legs.*

> Shit!

Something in SLOMO *changes.*

What?

SLOMO. I can see one, Buddy. You want me to shoot?

BUDDY. Got a good shot?

SLOMO *nods vigorously, an excited, strained, stifled noise accompanying the nod.*

Clean shot?

SLOMO *nods vigorously again, every fibre straining.*

No collateral?

SLOMO. Oh fuck, Buddy, you want me to shoot or not?

BUDDY *looks at the shit-stained cushion cover in his hands. He tosses it aside.*

BUDDY. Do it!

SLOMO *takes a quick shot, a couple of rounds at most. He spins away from the window as bullets are returned. He smiles at* BUDDY, *a look of extreme enthusiasm on his face. He gets to his feet. Paces a bit. A look of madness. Or glee. He makes a gesture towards the next room. It might incorporate a wanking gesture.*

SLOMO. I need to . . .

BUDDY. Yeah.

SLOMO *walks in a circle then heads towards the other room.*

Here. Don't forget your mother.

BUDDY *tosses the magazine to* SLOMO. SLOMO *catches it.*

SLOMO. Thanks, Buddy.

SLOMO *heads into the other room.* BUDDY *collapses onto the floor. For a second, lying there, trousers down, he looks post-orgasmic.* BUDDY *inspects his trousers as he rises.*

BUDDY. Oh, the fucking indignity.

BUDDY *pulls his trousers up and goes to the window. He glances out, seeing nothing of note.* BUDDY *wanders inside, picking through the occupants' private belongings. He finds an old record player and some LPs.*

Hey, we got music.

American shit.

Hey Slomo?

What kind of music you like?

SLOMO (*offstage*). Eh, I don't mind.

BUDDY. We got six or seven country and western albums and *Frampton Comes Alive!*

Slomo?

SLOMO (*offstage*). Eh, I can't really talk right now, Buddy.

BUDDY. Sorry. I forgot.

BUDDY *puts the needle down on a record. A burst of tinny heavy-metal guitar bursts out.* BUDDY *grimaces and pulls it off.*

SLOMO (*offstage*). Aw Buddy. Now I'm going to have to start all over again.

BUDDY. What you doing in there?

BUDDY *goes back to the window. Something he sees annoys him. He raises his gun and shoots a few bursts.* SLOMO *comes running through, pulling up his trousers as he comes, stumbling with his gun.* BUDDY *turns away from the window.* SLOMO *looks at him.*

Dogs. Kid you shot.

SLOMO. Aw Buddy . . .

BUDDY. Hey, I'm sorry. I'm sorry. Go finish.

BUDDY *sits down and puts his head in his hands.*

This is fucked up.

BUDDY *gets up and goes back to the record player. He selects one of the country records and puts it on. While his back is turned, a large* TEXAN *crawls through the mouse-hole. He is in his late middle age, immaculately dressed in cowboy casual, a large white Stetson hat setting off the ensemble.* BUDDY *catches this from the corner of his eye, jumping up, knocking over the record player as he grabs for his gun.* BUDDY *is spooked and confused. He fumbles in an effort to unlock his rifle, but manages. The* TEXAN'*s life is on a knife edge.*

Slomo!

SLOMO (*offstage*). Buddy!

BUDDY. Get out here now!

> *Part of* BUDDY *thinks this situation is all the record player's fault.*

SLOMO (*offstage*). Fuck off!

TEXAN. Easy, son. Easy. I'm a white man. Look.

> *The* TEXAN *takes his hat off to establish his racial ID.*

I'm with your army here. There's an Armenian right behind me with a couple of pips on his shoulder. He'll vouch.

> *The* TEXAN *makes a move towards the hole.*

BUDDY. Don't move!

TEXAN. Yossariat . . . I found me some live ones. You coming through?

YOSSARIAT (*offstage*). Coming through!

TEXAN. We're waiting, hoss. We're waiting.

> CAPTAIN YOSSARIAT *comes through the hole.* BUDDY *recognises him. His rifle never leaves the* TEXAN.

BUDDY. Yossariat. What the fuck's going on?

YOSSARIAT. What's not? You on your own?

BUDDY. Slomo's next door.

> YOSSARIAT *opens the door to the next room.*

YOSSARIAT. Slomo!

> Oh for.

> Some things you never want to see.

> SLOMO *comes running through, embarrassed, his clothes in disarray, the porn magazine under his arm.*

> SLOMO *sees the* TEXAN *and pulls up short. The magazine falls. He looks incredulous then gets very excited. He gravitates towards* BUDDY *like a shy kid to its mother.*

SLOMO. Is that?

> Is that George-Bush?

> BUDDY *smiles, stifling a giggle.* YOSSARIAT *turns away. The*

TEXAN *knows something funny has been said, but doesn't know what.*

TEXAN. What did he say?

YOSSARIAT. He wanted to know if you were George-Bush.

The TEXAN *is surprised and pleased.*

TEXAN. Hell no, son, and I hope I did not give that impression. I've had the pleasure of his company on many a fine evening, but no, son, I am not him.

BUDDY. What the hell is this? Is he for real?

YOSSARIAT *takes the opportunity to reload his pistol, before checking the window. The* TEXAN *has begun removing his boot, searching for a pebble or sand.*

TEXAN. Hell, son, everybody in Texas knows old Dubya. I myself used to be a habitué of his Hawaiian parties before I found the path. You like hashish, son? I'll tell you something. My president does. That man could empty a chillum with one suck of his chimplike mouth. You ain't got no idea the temptations that man succumbed to on the way to the light. Hell, I was a sinner, but that boy? He was pure sin.

SLOMO. What's he saying?

BUDDY. He says he's not George-Bush.

TEXAN. What's the deal, Yossarian? You got soldiers in your army don't speak God's American?

YOSSARIAT. Okay. 1. The language is called English.

2. Half the men in my command do not speak 'English'!

3. My name is Yossariat.

Yo-say-ray-at.

TEXAN. Hoss, hoss . . . I mean no offence. I don't know why that name is stuck in my mind.

BUDDY. Yossariat?

YOSSARIAT. There's a woman back there. I'm going back for her. Keep an eye on him. Friendly.

YOSSARIAT *and* BUDDY *exchange looks.* YOSSARIAT *shakes his head and ducks out.*

BUDDY. Slomo.

17

SLOMO seems fascinated by the TEXAN. BUDDY *nods towards the window and* SLOMO *goes to stand guard, but he can't take his eyes off the* TEXAN. *The* TEXAN *is making himself at home. He notices* SLOMO *and smiles.*

TEXAN. You just can't keep your eyes off me, can you, son?

What?

What is it?

Is it . . . ?

The hat?

You like my hat?

He likes my hat.

BUDDY *rolls his eyes.*

You like my hat.

Here. Try it.

You want to try it?

Go on. Try it.

Try it on.

The TEXAN *holds out the hat.* SLOMO *glances shyly. As* SLOMO *comes towards him, the* TEXAN *flicks it like a Frisbee.* SLOMO *laughs and jumps to catch it, delighted. He holds the hat, shyly. He doesn't know if he should put it on or not. The* TEXAN *takes the hat from* SLOMO.

Here.

The TEXAN *puts the hat on* SLOMO*'s head.*

There you go.

SLOMO *is delighted.*

Well, son, you're a cowboy now.

SLOMO *gets acclimatised to the hat, trying to find his reflection somewhere. He assumes a gunslinger's position and goes for the quick draw. He does this two or three times, then laughs. The* TEXAN *beams.*

I don't know.

Everywhere you go.

Everybody wants to be a cowboy.

SLOMO *gives the* TEXAN *a thumbs up.*

SLOMO. George-Bush.

TEXAN. Least you smell like a cowboy, son.

Old George smells sweeter than a pansy in Macy's lingerie department.

Even when he was drinking, that boy still managed to smell sweet.

He glances at SLOMO, *who is readying himself for a draw. The* TEXAN *does likewise. They draw. Chuckles.* SLOMO *goes to draw again. The* TEXAN *waves him away.*

Too fast for me, hoss. Too fast.

He turns to BUDDY *as he makes himself comfortable.*

He really thought I was the president?

BUDDY. Don't get too proud. He thought this slut was his mother.

BUDDY *tosses the porn magazine, which* SLOMO *has dropped, at the* TEXAN. *It lands at his feet. The* TEXAN *picks it up and puts it aside without looking at it.*

TEXAN. Son, you've got a fine-looking mother. And you'll almost certainly go to hell for seeing her like that.

SLOMO. What did he say?

BUDDY. He said your mother's a whore.

SLOMO*'s hand tightens on his gun.* BUDDY *shakes his head.*

So who's this woman?

TEXAN. Ah, the Rabbi's wife? The Rabbi's wife is feeling a little unwell. A stone thrown by one of your pocket mujahideen hit her pretty head and wounded her. It was left for me to carry her through your baying mobs with their stones and their guns to the comparative safety of Yossarian's arms.

BUDDY. Yo-say-ray-at.

TEXAN. My pardon. You'll like the Rabbi's wife.

The RABBI'S WIFE *is lit – her high heels kicked off, a pistol on her chest and a hip flask in her hand. A dead rat lies near by. She is drunk, possibly concussed. Her hair is matted with blood.*

I had the pleasure of her company over breakfast this morning. We share the same hotel. She has her mind set on the redemption of her people and the abjection of mine. She doesn't understand that her people's redemption is also my people's redemption. She certainly doesn't understand that her people's redemption and her people's abjection is one and the same thing.

BUDDY. What the fuck are you talking about?

TEXAN. Prophecy.

The TEXAN *stretches his legs.*

Oh, I realise to your soldier's ears all talk of this nature seems nothing more than riddles. But solving riddles is a passion of mine. As it is with the Rabbi's wife and the majority of our group.

BUDDY. What group?

TEXAN. Our group. The group I travel with.

BUDDY. CIA?

TEXAN. Hell no, son. Our group. Our tour group. We're holidaymakers, son. Vacationers. Tourists, who travel where we will.

BUDDY *can't believe it.*

Yes sir, here. In the land of flames. In this Gehenna I chose to spend my precious vacation time. As did the Rabbi's wife. Who I have to stress has no connection to me beyond that spurious co-joining over the breakfast table. In what was a busy hotel.

SLOMO. What's he saying?

BUDDY. I don't know. He's talking shit.

TEXAN. My name is Daniel.

BUDDY. Like Daniel Boone?

TEXAN. No, son. Like the prophet. Like the book.

BUDDY *turns away.*

BUDDY. This guy's getting on my fucking tits.

SLOMO. Who? George-Bush?

BUDDY. Yeah. George-Bush.

SLOMO. Who is he?

BUDDY. I don't know.

SLOMO. Is he here to stop the war?

BUDDY. We're the only ones who can stop the war.

SLOMO. Yeah.

BUDDY. We'll kill and kill until there's nobody left to kill.

SLOMO. Yeah.

BUDDY. Then what'll we do? Eh? Then what'll we do?

SLOMO. Go home.

BUDDY. Yeah. We'll go home. We'll go home. And we'll kill them too.

What do we do?

SLOMO. Keep shooting.

BUDDY. Yeah. Keep shooting 'til the gun's empty.

'Til all the guns are empty.

Keep shooting 'til every fucker's dead.

TEXAN. My, you boys sure are close. What is that language you're speaking?

BUDDY. You shut up and sit down. If the greaseballs don't get you, I sure as fuck will.

TEXAN. Hell, son, you don't want to be thinking those thoughts. I ain't one of your greaseballs you can torture on a whim. You harm one hair on my head and it'll be like you're spitting in the face of the Messiah. Hell, it'd be like shitting in Mr Sharon's hat and watching him put it on. And I'm talking before the stroke here. You might reach some momentary enjoyment, but hoss, you ain't gonna live too long.

BUDDY *and the* TEXAN *face off. It's* BUDDY *who backs down. He turns on* SLOMO.

BUDDY. Go and sit down.

SLOMO. I'm not tired.

BUDDY. Go!

BUDDY *takes the window, glowering back resentfully at the* TEXAN. *The* TEXAN *seems happy. He sits and waits. He leans towards* SLOMO.

TEXAN. You don't speak any English, do you, son?

SLOMO *just looks at him.*

That's a shame.

You look like a fine young man.

I would've enjoyed talking to you, I'm sure.

SLOMO. What's he saying?

BUDDY. Ignore him.

TEXAN. I'm a friend of your people, son. Not many are, but I am. Nothing would have given me more pleasure today than to sit with you and tell you all about my saviour, Jesus Christ. He said, 'Suffer little children to come unto me', and you, son, when I see you here, look to me like a little child. I can see in your eyes the innocence of your soul. It would have given me nothing but pleasure to sit here and tell you about my Lord. And you would have responded, I'm sure. There's a light in you, son. Maybe a light only I can see. But it's there. Language is the curse of mankind, son. It cleaves us asunder. We are one, and yet divided, and language is at that core. Can you imagine how wonderful it would be if we could sit here and talk, commune, man to man, one spirit to another.

SLOMO *is delighted. He turns to* BUDDY, *jerking his thumb back in the direction of the* TEXAN.

SLOMO. George-Bush.

SLOMO *purses his lips like an incontinent chimpanzee and flashes a victory sign. He looks around, moving his V-sign from left to right and back again, mock confusion on his face, then settles. He bursts out laughing. The* TEXAN *watches this, unsmiling.*

TEXAN. Yes, son. George Bush.

The TEXAN *takes the hat from* SLOMO's *head and meanders towards the mouse-hole.*

BUDDY. Hey! What you doing?

TEXAN. I was growing concerned about the Rabbi's wife.

It seems a long time since your captain went away.

BUDDY. Worry about yourself.

TEXAN. Son, I have nothing to worry about. No fear.

His sword is my sword. His shield my shield.

BUDDY *spots something out of the corner of his eye.*

BUDDY. Get down!

A Molotov cocktail explodes against the side of the house near the window. SLOMO rolls from his chair and comes up into a fighting stance. BUDDY slaps SLOMO's leg. SLOMO jumps into the window and empties a magazine into the street before jumping aside. BUDDY takes his place, not firing. The danger is gone. BUDDY collapses onto the floor. The TEXAN has barely flinched. He gets to his feet, brushing himself down. He goes to the window, plants his hands on the ledge and looks out.

TEXAN. The Lord is my shepherd, I shall not want.
He maketh me to lie down in green pastures.
He leadeth me beside still waters.
He restoreth my soul.

The TEXAN spreads his arms and smiles.

Lights.

TWO

The RABBI'S WIFE sits shivering and miserable in a corner of the room, her high heels kicked off, her beautiful clothes dirty and blooded. Blood mats her hair. She talks through her fever.

RABBI'S WIFE. You know who else hates the Jews?

Uh?

Bibi?

Rich people.

Oh God, you should hear the speckled wrens of privilege sing!

Those little twittering daughters of the Republic!

You know how sick America is?

Uh?

Don't ever go to America.

They put me in a school.

My parents?

This cunt-shrivelling Bedford pukka pukka white-girl school.

I tell you.

If you should ever have children.

If you should ever.

Better send them to a whore house than a bastion of.

A bastion of.

What's the word?

YOSSARIAT. Decency?

The RABBI'S WIFE *laughs.*

RABBI'S WIFE. Decency.

I would have gone back there.

I would have gone back there with an Uzi if I had had an Uzi back then.

Like those kids in Columbine.

Those fucking heroes.

Like Baruch Goldstein, who walked into the Tomb of the Patriarchs with his Galil rifle and shot them down, one by one by one.

All the way to twenty-nine.

She tries to push herself up, but fails.

Now he was a Jew.

Another American familiar with the cold heart of privilege.

Why did he come here you think?

Why did he care?

Didn't he know what shit heap.

A shit hole.

It was.

A repository for shit that needs divided.

I will build a wall between my shit and your shit!

Our shit must not touch!

SLOMO *is guarding the window,* BUDDY *and the* TEXAN *are nowhere to be seen.* YOSSARIAT *goes to her, picking up her shoes.*

YOSSARIAT. Come on, there's a bed next door.

RABBI'S WIFE. No!

Not another step.

I'm sick of it.

Fucking.

Walking these. Desert streets.

I will stay here until the Messiah comes or my bones are returned to the desert.

The desert shall have me.

Hosanna!

She flings out her arms, catching YOSSARIAT*'s face. The sight of the dejected soldier cheers the* RABBI'S WIFE. *She laughs.*

Oh Yossariat, why so sad?

We walk the streets God gave us.

Aren't you enjoying it?

YOSSARIAT. Oh, you fucked-up bitch of hell!

When Satan fucked you he left a piece of his dick up your arse!

Didn't he?

Didn't he?

The RABBI'S WIFE *laughs.*

RABBI'S WIFE. What is that?

Russian?

Some barbaric, guttural Slav monkey noise.

Listen to me.

Don't speak that language in front of me again.

I mean it.

Not another word.

You treat me with respect.

I demand that you treat me with respect.

YOSSARIAT *sits beside her, admirably in control, despite his desire to strangle her.*

YOSSARIAT. Madam. All day long I have shown you nothing but respect. This morning when I picked you up from your hotel, I showed you nothing but respect. When I accompanied your party against my better judgement to a part of the city you had no right to be in, I showed you nothing but respect. When I stood back and watched as you picked up that first brick and threw it through the greaseball baker's window, I showed you nothing but respect. When I watched your colleagues follow suit and also pick up bricks and also destroy property, I showed you nothing but respect. And when I watched your fellow travellers take sticks to that quiet, gentle old man and beat him and punch him and kick him and spit on him – when you tore the clothes from his equally elderly wife and laughed and barked at her humiliation and his, though my heart was breaking and my hands wanted to murder each and every one of you, I showed you nothing but respect. Even when the gunshots started and I was forced to order my men to shoot back, indiscriminately, to shoot into children, children like my own, as I watched those children fall one by one, still I showed you nothing but respect. Even as the tears were running down my face, as the fires began to engulf us, as we ran, still shooting, I protecting you, I showed you nothing but respect. I have done my duty to protect you even though the shame I feel is choking me and drowning me and humiliating me. I have shown you nothing but respect.

The RABBI'S WIFE *laughs. Her fingers brush his cheek lovingly.*

RABBI'S WIFE. Oh Bibi.

You silly little man.

You're a disgrace to that uniform.

The uniform of martyrs, and you disgrace it.

She settles down to sleep where she sits.

YOSSARIAT. Get up.

Get up!

YOSSARIAT *pulls her to her feet. The* RABBI'S WIFE *struggles.*

RABBI'S WIFE. No!

Stop it!

I'm not some greaseball village you can just bulldozer your way through.

I have.

Her mouth opens in agony.

YOSSARIAT. You have a piece of glass in your foot.

The RABBI'S WIFE *hops to a seat.*

RABBI'S WIFE. Yes. I have a piece of glass in my foot.

And you have an internship at Kesher Barel you are desperately keen to hold on to.

Don't you?

Eh?

You see.

I know you.

Brave Captain Yossariat.

I know your wife too.

How is it to live with a lesbian, tell me?

Do they smell?

Of course she wasn't always a lesbian, was she, Yossariat?

A cock-hungry slut, her mother called her.

The best psychiatrists in Tel Aviv couldn't cure her of her cravings.

But you could.

What's your secret, eh Bibi?

Did you start it all, huh?

Did you lick her pussy, Yossariat?

Did you give her the taste?

The TEXAN *appears at the mouse-hole followed by* BUDDY.
The TEXAN *has a talking Mickey Mouse doll in his hand.*

TEXAN. Hey, you made it.

Look what I found.

He pulls Mickey's string. YOSSARIAT *snaps.*

YOSSARIAT. Get him out of here.

> *The* TEXAN *isn't having that. He struggles against* BUDDY*'s persuasion.*

TEXAN. Hey, wait a minute.

> What happened to her foot?

RABBI'S WIFE. He pushed me.

> He stole my shoes and made me walk on glass.

> I have witnesses.

YOSSARIAT. She stood on glass.

RABBI'S WIFE. The liar. He tortured me. He beat me. He cut me.

> *The* TEXAN *gets pushed back.*

BUDDY. Slomo!

> SLOMO *turns his gun on the* TEXAN, *who backs off.*

> I don't know what your game is today, Yossariat, but you're turning my war into a fucking circus.

YOSSARIAT. Hey, my war's not everything it could be either. Trust me.

RABBI'S WIFE. War?

> This isn't a war?

> All you've got to do is hang on to land better men than you already conquered.

> Do you think you could do that?

> Do you?

YOSSARIAT. We'll certainly try.

RABBI'S WIFE. Look at my dress.

> This morning I dressed for dignity.

> We bring civilisation to the desert.

> Paris fashions. Endless freeways. Things not to be despised.

> If I gave this blouse to a greaseball she'd wear it for a turban.

> A death veil.

> A death veil.

A death veil.

She makes the call of mourning that is common amongst Muslim women and laughs. YOSSARIAT *sits with his head in his hands.*

BUDDY. Do you know who that is?

YOSSARIAT *nods.*

YOSSARIAT. Look after George Bush.

RABBI'S WIFE. George Bush?

Don't talk to me about George Bush.

Blacks he sends to talk to us.

Blacks.

SLOMO *is staring at the* RABBI'S WIFE.

BUDDY. Slomo!

SLOMO *goes to cover the* TEXAN. BUDDY *goes to dress the* RABBI'S WIFE*'s foot.*

If Madame will allow.

YOSSARIAT. Buddy?

BUDDY. You're fucking with strong medicine here, Yossariat.

This bitch can get you killed.

RABBI'S WIFE. Again with the monkey noises.

BUDDY. My pardon.

RABBI'S WIFE. Not you.

That.

That cuckold.

Look at him.

She takes a swig from her hip flask. It is empty.

What a shit hole this country is.

She looks around for a replacement drink. She sees BUDDY *trying to bandage her rarely still foot.*

You?

What's your name?

BUDDY. Buddy.

RABBI'S WIFE. Buddy?

> BUDDY *nods. The* RABBI'S WIFE *remembers a line from a David Bowie song.*

> 'His name was always Buddy, and he'd shrug and ask to stay . . . '

BUDDY. Yeah, that's me.

RABBI'S WIFE. Buddy.

> His name was always Buddy.

> You look like a man who can get things done.

> I need whisky and a place to lie down where it's quiet.

> My head hurts.

> I'm surrounded by perverts and degenerates.

> Can you do that for me?

> Can you find me a bottle of whisky and a place to lay my head?

> YOSSARIAT*'s body language is screaming – Don't you dare.* BUDDY *considers his options and nods.*

BUDDY. I can do that for you.

YOSSARIAT. Buddy?

RABBI'S WIFE. I love you for that.

> BUDDY *lifts her.*

> What?

> What are you doing?

BUDDY. It's okay.

> You're safe.

> *She puts her fingers on his chest.*

RABBI'S WIFE. This is a man's chest.

> Not a little pigeon chest.

> A man's chest.

YOSSARIAT. Buddy?

RABBI'S WIFE. Samson.

> Goliath.

Solomon.

David.

Buddy?

She laughs.

Buddy.

She buries into BUDDY*'s shoulder as the others look on.*

Lights.

THREE

YOSSARIAT *sits in a foul mood, trying to get some joy out of a defective radio/walkie-talkie.* SLOMO *is at the window, still fascinated by the* TEXAN. *The* TEXAN *is also by the window.*

TEXAN. Lord, I love that view. Even with all that smoke. It truly is miraculous.

You won't remember '67, will you, son?

Wouldn't even've been born.

I remember.

I remember watching it. Watching it on TV.

Back in.

Back in Texas.

Course I wasn't much interested back then.

I was a young man. I had bigger fish to fry.

Daddy though?

When the news came through that Jerusalem had fallen.

I still remember him.

He turned to me and said:

'Son – what you have just heard is the single most important piece of information that box has ever conveyed to the human race; and it'll stay that way until old Walter Cronkite comes on to announce that Jesus Christ himself is alive and well and walking amongst us again.'

Daddy knew prophecy.

I didn't.

Not then.

You had to be impressed though.

A man like that.

A man you'd admired and respected and feared your whole life.

Saying a thing like that.

And believing it.

The tears of belief. Running down his cheek.

There's things that need to happen, see.

Before Jesus comes.

Before this corrupt world can end and God's reign on earth begin.

Before Jesus Christ can return.

Things, yep. And not one of them had happened by the time I was a child.

It's been humbling, I tell you, to watch in my lifetime piece after piece fall into place.

To realise that the Bible – which I'd always taken as a sop for children – was in fact history.

The things that had been.

The things that would be.

That every word.

Was.

Literally.

True.

It'll be hard on your people, I know.

I won't kid you, hoss.

What's coming up ain't gonna be a particularly nice time for the Jew.

Tribulation like you've never seen before.

And the Jew has seen much tribulation.

I ain't exactly a theologian, see.

My place in this is more as a facilitator.

But my friends who know tell me that the coming days will be very unpleasant for the.

Unconverted. Jew. And I'm sorry for that.

I really am.

I guess a lot of people are going to die when the end comes.

SLOMO *approaches the* TEXAN.

SLOMO. Want to swap?

The TEXAN *smiles, still fanning the hat.*

TEXAN. What's that, son?

The TEXAN *gestures that he doesn't understand.* SLOMO *looks around for stuff to swap.*

SLOMO. Swap.

I've got . . . I've got.

He grabs up his porn magazine. He looks at the TEXAN *and considers for a second. He doesn't really want to lose the magazine. He proffers the magazine in the* TEXAN's *direction.*

TEXAN. What? I don't want that.

SLOMO. Here. Take it.

TEXAN. No.

SLOMO. Go on.

TEXAN. Stop it now . . . Just . . . Stop it!

The TEXAN *slaps the magazine out of* SLOMO's *hand.*

I don't want that filth.

SLOMO *looks hurt, angry. He turns away from the* TEXAN. *Then turns back.*

SLOMO. I want that hat!

SLOMO *makes a grab for the hat. The* TEXAN *jumps back.*

TEXAN. Now don't!

SLOMO. I want that hat!

YOSSARIAT *loses patience.*

YOSSARIAT. Oh, just give him the fucking hat!

The shocked TEXAN *drops the hat.* SLOMO *scoops it up when the* TEXAN's *back is turned. The* TEXAN *is angered, but waves it away.*

TEXAN. Hell, son, you want the hat, you keep the hat.

Ain't as if it's my favourite or nothing.

The TEXAN *retreats to his seat. He casts dark glances at* SLOMO.

I know this might sound a bit rich, coming from a Texan and everything.

But you really think that boy should have a gun?

YOSSARIAT. I don't see why not.

The TEXAN *can think of a few reasons.*

He's a killer.

He wouldn't be much good at his chosen profession if he didn't have a gun.

Now, would he?

TEXAN. He's a killer?

YOSSARIAT. Yes.

He's a killer.

He's a great killer.

SLOMO *realises he's being talked about.*

TEXAN. He's a boy.

YOSSARIAT *shrugs.*

You ever thought about what's going to happen to him?

I mean afterwards? When he gets back home?

YOSSARIAT. I don't see anything good in his future.

Do you?

SLOMO *is enjoying the hat.* YOSSARIAT *gives him a fond look. He smiles.*

TEXAN. So how long you think we'll be stuck here?

Captain?

Captain?

YOSSARIAT. Why don't you ask your tour guide?

Or didn't they give you an itinerary at the hotel this morning?

TEXAN. Well, this morning.

This morning was a little 'off reservation', if you know what I mean?

YOSSARIAT. Oh, I don't know.

It looked pretty 'on reservation' to me.

In fact I'd say you walked straight into the centre of their reservation and pissed all over their totem pole.

But then what do I know? Eh?

I'm only here to clear up your mess.

Not define it.

TEXAN. This doesn't have to be difficult, you know?

YOSSARIAT. No. I realise that.

And yet?

His upturned palm suggests it is out of his control.

TEXAN. It's easy to be bitter, son.

Hell, I remember when.

YOSSARIAT *stops him with a look.*

Don't matter.

I can see you're busy.

BUDDY *emerges from the other room and closes the door.*

Oh soldier?

Soldier?

How's the lady?

YOSSARIAT. Yes, how is Madama Macbeth?

BUDDY *goes to sit with* YOSSARIAT.

BUDDY. You just don't know how to talk to women, Yossariat.

That's your problem.

YOSSARIAT *laughs.*

You okay there, cowboy?

SLOMO. Sky's on.

Sky's on fire.

BUDDY *takes a bottle of the whisky from his backpack.*
YOSSARIAT *looks up.*

YOSSARIAT. What you doing?

BUDDY. Lady wants a drink.

YOSSARIAT. So?

BUDDY. So a hundred dollars American says she can have one.

BUDDY *flashes the money.*

YOSSARIAT. That's one way to tame a wild dog, I suppose.

Get down on your hands and knees and sniff its arsehole.

SLOMO *laughs. He stops when they look.*

BUDDY. You still don't get this, do you, Yossariat?

BUDDY *gets close to get his point across.*

They will petrol fill a tyre and pop it round your head.

You'll still feel it.

Long after you're dead you'll feel it.

That rubber will burn through your flesh long after you've
passed on.

BUDDY *nods gravely – Think on.* YOSSARIAT *issues a shrug
of denial, trying his best to avoid* BUDDY*'s eyes.*

Oh.

She said to tell you.

Your internship's just come to an abrupt end.

That mean anything to you?

YOSSARIAT *vaguely shakes his head, trying to avoid*
BUDDY*'s eyes. He bites his lip and holds his nose as if a
migraine is coming on.*

Good.

The RABBI'S WIFE *appears in the doorway.*

RABBI'S WIFE. Buddy? We had a deal.

YOSSARIAT*'s head jerks up at the sound of her voice.* BUDDY *reacts to this.*

BUDDY. I think Captain Yossariat would prefer it if you stayed in the other room.

The RABBI'S WIFE *takes the bottle from his hand.*

RABBI'S WIFE. And does Captain Yossariat own Israel?

No.

Then Captain Yossariat can fuck off.

She grabs the bottle from BUDDY*'s hand and sits. She opens the bottle and sniffs.*

A toast.

To my new friend.

His name was always Buddy.

Let his obituary read – He came through.

When the chips were down, he was the man.

The delivery guy.

Cheers!

BUDDY. Come on.

RABBI'S WIFE. No, why should I?

Is it my fault he can't fuck his wife properly?

Did I make his wife a degenerate?

Did I?

YOSSARIAT. You've got quite a foul mouth. For a Rabbi's wife.

RABBI'S WIFE. Fuck you.

I've got a clean soul.

BUDDY *takes a step back. The* RABBI'S WIFE *is instantly apologetic.*

Ah Buddy.

I'm sorry.

They don't understand.

In the time of the Messiah, everything is permitted.

Mmmnh?

There is no sin.

No morality.

It's a sign of the Saviour.

That the Saviour is coming.

Unholiness.

Maybe that's why the captain's wife has changed?

Mmmn?

Maybe she senses the time is approaching.

She knows the time is right.

Or maybe she's just a pervert.

Who knows?

YOSSARIAT *is close to breaking point.*

Aw Bibi.

Look at your face.

Did I do that?

Is that my fault?

BUDDY *tries to get her next door.*

BUDDY. Come on. Let's get you next door.

RABBI'S WIFE. Ah Buddy, it doesn't matter. It's our time. God is
  smiling.

BUDDY. I bet he is.

But my face is deadly serious.

RABBI'S WIFE. Oh Buddy.

I get so tired looking at you.

I feel young, but it makes me tired.

BUDDY. Go to sleep then.

RABBI'S WIFE. Will you come with me?

BUDDY *shakes his head.*

Aw Buddy.

Please.

Just hold me, please.

Hold me until I fall.

Hold my hand until I'm over.

Can you do that for me?

Just hold my hand.

TEXAN. Do you really think she should be drinking, Captain?

Captain?

YOSSARIAT *isn't taking any calls right now. The* TEXAN
approaches BUDDY *and the* RABBI'S WIFE *who have not
moved. The* TEXAN *thinks getting the bottle off the* RABBI'S
WIFE *might be a good idea.*

My dear, do you really think you should be?

Please, that was a nasty knock you.

RABBI'S WIFE. Who is this?

This?

Pooka?

BUDDY. I think you had breakfast with him.

RABBI'S WIFE. No, I had breakfast with an interesting man this
morning.

A temple builder.

What is it about these Americans and their temples?

Always.

Building them.

Blowing them up.

TEXAN. My dear. Ssssshhh!

You've taken a knock to the head.

You're traumatised.

Captain? I really think she should be in hospital.

The RABBI'S WIFE*'s body language says – Who is this clown?*

RABBI'S WIFE. Don't shush me.

Who is this?

This man?

TEXAN. My dear.

I'm Daniel Pendleton, ma'am, from Wesley, Texas.

We talked on the phone you might recall.

And today at breakfast.

The RABBI'S WIFE *sees* SLOMO's *hat. She looks from the hat on* SLOMO's *head to the* TEXAN *and back.*

RABBI'S WIFE. Didn't you . . .

She describes a hat with her finger in the air. The TEXAN *smiles.*

TEXAN. Now we're getting somewhere.

Something clicks into place. The RABBI'S WIFE *grabs his arm and pulls him towards her, her nails digging in.*

RABBI'S WIFE. Did I not tell you this morning to rub your nose in my hole and never come back to me again?

Didn't I?

Did I not tell you to rub your nose in my hole?

The RABBI'S WIFE *drags her nails down his arm. The* TEXAN *jumps back, perhaps bleeding.* BUDDY *grabs the* RABBI'S WIFE.

Let me tell you again.

Rub your nose in my hole and never come back to me again.

Are we clear?

Rub your nose in my hole.

TEXAN. She's delirious. She's been hit on the head.

BUDDY. Come on now.

RABBI'S WIFE. No, I remember it quite clearly.

You were following me.

TEXAN. No.

RABBI'S WIFE. Yes.

This man has been following me around for weeks.

He's like the flu. I can't shake him off.

TEXAN. My dear, you've had a.

RABBI'S WIFE. I was assaulted. By terrorists. Were you there?

Yes.

And we had breakfast together this morning?

TEXAN. There you go.

I knew she'd remember.

Had me worried there.

RABBI'S WIFE. This man has been following me.

Ask him why he's been following me!

Ask him!

The RABBI'S WIFE *goes for the* TEXAN. *The* TEXAN *jumps back.*

TEXAN. This is crazy.

She invited me.

My dear.

It was you who invited me. Remember?

RABBI'S WIFE. I invited you to the desert?

To die?

TEXAN. Well, not in so many words.

YOSSARIAT, *who has been trying to raise a signal on his radio, bounces the radio off the floor.*

YOSSARIAT. PIECE OF SHIT!

What do you have to do in this army to get a radio that fucking works?

He distractedly picks up, or tries to pick up, the broken radio as the others look on.

I bet we bought them off the fucking British!

Fucking unbelievable!

He turns to the TEXAN.

You want electricals who do you go to?

You know?

In the shop?

What make?

What brand?

What nationality?

Tell me!

The TEXAN *shrugs.*

TEXAN. Japanese?

YOSSARIAT. Yes!

See!

Exactly!

So why the fuck . . .

The TEXAN *and* SLOMO *are both looking at* YOSSARIAT.

Oh, forget it. Forget it.

We'll stay here.

Why not?

It's a fucking freak show but it's entertaining enough.

TEXAN. We can't just stay here.

YOSSARIAT. Oh, I'm sorry.

Did you have a pressing engagement somewhere else?

TEXAN. Well, I did have a meeting.

YOSSARIAT. Well, you should have thought about that before you started throwing bricks through people's windows.

Shouldn't you?

Hoss.

TEXAN. Now wait a minute, captain. I was not involved in any of that.

YOSSARIAT. Slomo? Where's that wank mag?

YOSSARIAT *looks. He spots it under the* TEXAN*'s chair and goes to pick it up.*

TEXAN. Now wait a minute, captain . . .

YOSSARIAT. Wait a minute what!

YOSSARIAT tosses the magazine down. His violent movement spooks SLOMO. He swings round and unlocks his rifle. The gun is pointed at the TEXAN.

TEXAN. Hey. Easy now.

The RABBI'S WIFE finds this all very amusing.

RABBI'S WIFE. You'll have to excuse Captain Yossariat.

He's having a stressful day.

YOSSARIAT. Get her out of here.

Now.

BUDDY pulls the RABBI'S WIFE away. YOSSARIAT grabs the whisky bottle from her. The RABBI'S WIFE laughs.

RABBI'S WIFE. Did I make his wife a degenerate?

Did I?

Did I?

YOSSARIAT curls up in a corner with the whisky and the porn mag. The TEXAN is still facing down the barrel of SLOMO's gun.

Lights.

FOUR

YOSSARIAT sits in a world of his own. SLOMO watches the fire outside, humming to himself 'Burn, Motherfucker, Burn' by Metallica. The TEXAN is becoming increasingly worried by SLOMO and his soft, psychotic singing. The elements and the exertions of the day are also beginning to take their toll on his ageing body. He sighs.

YOSSARIAT. Slomo, stop that will you please, there's a good chap.

We're not Americans.

TEXAN. Thank you.

BUDDY comes out, holding the whisky bottle. YOSSARIAT grabs it from him and returns to his perch. BUDDY joins him.

BUDDY. Rough day, soldier?

YOSSARIAT. I have not slept for more than one hour in seven days.

I have chewed so much caffeine my teeth have turned to ice.

I'm this close to killing someone.

Just for the fuck of it.

YOSSARIAT *looks at the cigarette in his hand, shakes his head and pushes it onto* BUDDY.

Here.

I've quit.

YOSSARIAT *takes the whisky and gets to his feet.* BUDDY *watches* YOSSARIAT.

TEXAN. Soldier?

Oh soldier?

The TEXAN *indicates towards the other room.*

BUDDY. She's sleeping.

YOSSARIAT *turns away, disgusted that the* RABBI'S WIFE *can sleep and he cannot. He takes his gun out, busying himself with the mechanisms, trying to distract and calm himself with routine.*

TEXAN. Sleeping?

YOSSARIAT'*s gun clicks loudly back into place.*

The sleep of innocence.

I wish I was innocent.

BUDDY. It's the whisky that's sleeping, Yossariat.

That bitch'll never sleep another honest night again.

YOSSARIAT'*s control of the gun becomes more erratic. He slams it down.*

YOSSARIAT. Why not?

Maybe she's right.

Maybe God wants us to kill kids.

Infidel kids.

Maybe every little bastard we shoot *is* us one step closer to redemption.

BUDDY *smirks.*

BUDDY. I feel redemption.

Their eyes meet. YOSSARIAT *nods.*

YOSSARIAT. I too.

I too feel redemption.

YOSSARIAT *slumps into a chair.*

What makes a person like that, do you think?

Poison.

Just poison.

I don't understand these people, Buddy.

BUDDY *begins rolling a joint. He nods for* SLOMO *to keep watching the street.*

I mean.

We've all been fighting greaseballs since we were eighteen, more or less.

We don't take it personally.

I mean.

I don't take it personally.

Do you?

Take it personally?

BUDDY. If I was them I'd be fighting us too.

YOSSARIAT. Yes.

Exactly.

We see the rationale.

She?

There's nothing rational about her, is there?

This morning.

This tour group.

She just leads them straight up into greaseball heaven.

Not a care in the world.

And she encourages them to start throwing.

Bricks.

I mean?

Tourists?

Who are they, these Europeans?

These Americans?

These foreigners?

Who are they to come to this country. And vandalise it?

TEXAN. Captain.

> BUDDY*'s eyes are on the* TEXAN. YOSSARIAT *has more to drink.*

BUDDY. They love it, don't they?

> The fires.

> Breaking glass.

> That whole Kristallnacht vibe.

> YOSSARIAT *laughs.*

> Still. Must be nice for them.

> Being on top for once.

YOSSARIAT. Oh, I know they're victims.

> I understand they're persecuted.

> I've even heard in some of those backward old countries our kinsmen are reduced to driving S-series Mercs.

> I understand the indignity they must feel.

> Their thirst for revenge.

> She's different though.

> That one.

BUDDY. She's no shrinking violet, is she?

> YOSSARIAT *shakes his head.*

TEXAN. Captain.

> YOSSARIAT *rounds on the meddlesome* TEXAN.

YOSSARIAT. Are you still here?

TEXAN. Yes.

YOSSARIAT. Why?

I mean.

What are you doing here?

I mean what are you doing here?

Strutting around in that stupid, ridiculous outfit?

Who are you supposed to be?

Roy Rogers?

Trigger?

Oh, who was the cowboy and who was the horse?

Trigger?

Fucking Trigger?

TEXAN. Roy Rogers was the cowboy.

YOSSARIAT. I know Roy Rogers is the cowboy.

I'm not a fucking retard.

I just happen to be having a particularly stressful day escorting you and your bunch of homicidal Jew Nazis around my charming, slightly rowdy town.

So please?

Just tell me?

What are you doing here?

What the fuck do you want?

The TEXAN *looks at him with sad eyes.*

TEXAN. I don't want nothing but to go home, son.

I want to go to my hotel room and take my washcloth from my TWA bag, soak it in cold water, and lay it on my face.

I want the familiar comfort of a Sheraton double bed.

It's been a long day.

He sees YOSSARIAT *go back to the whisky.*

And liquor ain't the answer, son.

Don't matter what the question, that ain't the answer.

BUDDY *has watched all this with a cold eye. His focus is on*
YOSSARIAT.

BUDDY. Still.

I bet she'd be the ride of your life.

YOSSARIAT *is delighted by the unexpectedness of this, first not*
understanding, then understanding.

YOSSARIAT. I bet she'd be a fucking tiger!

YOSSARIAT *ponders this.* YOSSARIAT *feels* BUDDY*'s eyes*
on him. He sees BUDDY*'s smile.*

What?

BUDDY. Try it.

YOSSARIAT. What?

With her?

You're out of your mind.

BUDDY. You're Para.

YOSSARIAT. So?

BUDDY. Para fuck anything.

It's what you're famous for.

SLOMO *leans in whispering.*

SLOMO. Are we going to fuck her?

BUDDY *ignores him, his attention on* YOSSARIAT.

YOSSARIAT. I certainly wouldn't leave me alone in the same
room as your wife again, that's for sure.

Still. Must be nice. Having a woman like that? Eh?

One who moans so much.

BUDDY. I'm not married.

YOSSARIAT. Oh, sorry, was that pretty lady your mother?

She told me she was your wife.

I thought at the time – bit mature for Buddy. But maybe he's
liberal like that.

Besides.

He's no oil painting himself.

Maybe this is the best he can afford.

BUDDY. My mother's dead.

YOSSARIAT. Yes. I know.

But least she died with a smile on her face.

Eh?

BUDDY. I wouldn't be surprised.

She was going down on your wife at the time.

YOSSARIAT *has to admit that was funny.* BUDDY*'s good at this.*

TEXAN. Captain?

YOSSARIAT. You go.

BUDDY. Think I want Satan's sloppy seconds?

YOSSARIAT *is delighted by the childishness of this. He repeats it to himself.*

YOSSARIAT. You've got a point.

You are spot-fucking-on!

What man in his right mind would go near a woman after Satan's FUCKED HER UP THE ARSE!

It can only end in disappointment!

The TEXAN *can't understand the language, but he's getting worried nonetheless.*

TEXAN. Excuse me.

Captain?

Captain?

YOSSARIAT. What?

TEXAN. Are you talking about the lady?

YOSSARIAT. Yes, we were as a matter of fact.

Would you care to contribute?

TEXAN. Only to say that she's had a hard life. That maybe a little forgiveness is in order.

YOSSARIAT. Forgiveness?

The way you forgave Fallujah?

BUDDY *laughs, despite himself.*

TEXAN. Her husband was killed.

Gunned down on a street corner.

YOSSARIAT. Yes. In New York of all places.

By a righteous Mohammedan gun.

TEXAN. I wouldn't call any gun used in the slaying of a man of God righteous.

YOSSARIAT. Even a man of God with an interest in politics?

A man of God who threatened to declare war on every greaseball nation the moment he attained power?

Who wanted to declare sexual relations between the races a capital offence?

Who wanted to use captured greaseball terrorists for medical experiments?

Medical experiments?

Do you have no memory?

TEXAN. He was still a man of God.

YOSSARIAT. Then God should keep better company.

Oh, I tell you. There. There was a man whose hand I would like to shake.

The righteous greaseball with the righteous gun that sent the righteous Rabbi to hell. To the hottest hell.

BUDDY. It wasn't a greaseball.

YOSSARIAT. What?

BUDDY. We did it.

YOSSARIAT. Did we?

BUDDY. I know a guy who knows the guy.

YOSSARIAT *makes a shooting gesture.*

YOSSARIAT. Does she know?

BUDDY *shrugs.*

BUDDY. I know.

YOSSARIAT. Fuck.

That would probably make me bitter as well.

BUDDY *and* YOSSARIAT *break into laughter.*

SLOMO. What?

BUDDY. Nothing. We're talking about the bitch.

SLOMO. Are we going to fuck her?

BUDDY. She's a bitch. Forget about her.

YOSSARIAT. Maybe later, eh? She's sleeping now.

SLOMO *turns back to the window, disappointed.*

TEXAN. You're wrong about the Rabbi, son. The Rabbi was a
great man.

YOSSARIAT. The Rabbi was a fucking maniac.

A Nazi scumbag. And his wife's no better.

BUDDY. Worse.

YOSSARIAT. Yes, worse.

Little fucking Evita.

What's her game?

What's she doing back here?

Eh?

TEXAN. Ask her.

YOSSARIAT. I'm asking you.

TEXAN. How would I know?

YOSSARIAT. I don't know. But I feel there's a connection.

TEXAN. I did meet him a couple of times.

The Rabbi.

He came to our church.

Ten thousand Christians turned out to hear him speak.

That's a measure of the man.

Ten thousand.

YOSSARIAT. Ten thousand? That's a big church.

TEXAN. We don't do small in Texas.

YOSSARIAT. No. Of course not.

You ever ask yourself why?

Do you?

Is it because a small thing needs careful examination?

You've got to look really hard to see what it is.

And you don't like that, do you?

You want it IN YOUR FACE!

Preferably in black and white.

Preferably in white.

I'm guessing you're not one of nature's questioners.

Are you, Mr Texas?

TEXAN. I've questioned just about everything about my life, son.

What you don't like is that my questions were answered.

YOSSARIAT. I wish mine were.

TEXAN. They can be.

YOSSARIAT. Are you . . . ? Are you trying to convert me?

TEXAN. The answers are all there in that book.

He indicates the discarded Bible. YOSSARIAT *picks it up.*

YOSSARIAT. What? This? Let me see, let me see? No.

Can't see anything.

Can you?

He tosses the Bible to BUDDY. *Something about his body language – an element of over-control or under-control – suggests he is gearing up to really fuck somebody up.*

BUDDY. What's the question?

YOSSARIAT. Oh, I've got more than one. Let's start with what Tex Ritter's doing in my country? Wearing this stupid, ridiculous hat?

YOSSARIAT *grabs the hat off* SLOMO'*s head and throws it contemptuously onto the* TEXAN. SLOMO'*s not too pleased. The* TEXAN *allows it to bounce off his body.*

BUDDY. How about it, Tex?

Want to answer that one?

TEXAN. Son, you are making a big mistake here.

YOSSARIAT. Are we?

TEXAN. I'm a friend of your government's.

A good friend!

YOSSARIAT. Oh, I know that.

I know you're a friend of my government's.

That's the reason I've been following you step by step through this entire shitty nightmare.

I have been ordered to give my life to preserve yours. And I'll do it. I will.

Because I am loyal.

I am a fucking stand-up guy.

If I say I'm going to do something, I jolly well do it.

But hoss, you making it hard, boy.

You making it so hard.

BUDDY. Chill, Yossariat.

Take a smoke.

YOSSARIAT. I told you. I've quit.

TEXAN. Thank you.

YOSSARIAT. What?

TEXAN. Thank you.

For protecting me.

Appreciate it.

The TEXAN *holds out his hand.* YOSSARIAT *is stunned. Flabbergasted even. He disingenuously waves away the thanks.*

YOSSARIAT. No, really. Don't mention it.

My pleasure.

He doesn't take the TEXAN'*s hand.*

Fuck, I hope the Hindus are right and I come back as an American.

You can't beat that.

He sniffs. He turns to see the joint in BUDDY*'s mouth.*

Is that?

BUDDY. All the way from the Free Lebanon.

YOSSARIAT *takes the joint and looks at it.*

YOSSARIAT. Oh Buddy, you're just full of surprises.

YOSSARIAT *takes a deep draw. It reminds him of something sad. He looks at the joint, takes a few more puffs. It does no good. He gives it back to* BUDDY *who offers it to* SLOMO *who declines.* YOSSARIAT *sits. He's never looked more exhausted in his life.*

Do you ever get sick of this?

I do.

And then I go home, and I've got to admit it.

I love it out here.

I love it.

I got married to this woman – this debutante – and fuck, she was gorgeous.

But her family.

Her family.

She has a fucking wonderful family.

But they own half the hotels in Eilat.

You know how much it costs to run a hooker like that?

And she's a lesbian. Did I mention that?

And no, before you ask, she doesn't let me watch.

I don't think she's even a lesbian.

I think she just pretends to be to fuck me off.

And I married this woman.

Smashed a glass.

And I am a man of my word.

BUDDY. Why don't we just go?

YOSSARIAT. We can't.

I'm not taking those two out on the streets before the piccaninnies go to bed.

I'm charged with their safety.

And I know nobody else gives a fuck about the honour of this army but I do.

And I obey orders.

I obey orders. You know?

BUDDY. We're the most moral army in the world.

YOSSARIAT. Yes. Yes.

YOSSARIAT *considers the joint in his hand. He takes a puff and stretches to pass it to* BUDDY.

You can't smoke pot in a war zone.

It's a proven fact.

Imagine if you have a white-out with a machine gun in your hands?

That's how wars start, isn't it?

BUDDY. War's started, mate.

YOSSARIAT. Good.

Good.

TEXAN. I know what you're doing, you know?

I may be old but even I recognise the distinctive aroma of primo Lebanese.

BUDDY. You want me to put it out?

TEXAN. Please.

He gets up and moves towards the TEXAN.

BUDDY. You must have a fucking huge dick?

Either that or you've overdosed on fucking lithium.

The joint in his hand burns menacingly close to the TEXAN's *face.*

You want me to put it out? Eh?

You want me to put it out?

YOSSARIAT *looks up, bored.*

YOSSARIAT. Buddy?

He's in my charge.

The TEXAN *pushes him away.* BUDDY *laughs.*

TEXAN. I'm not scared of you.

BUDDY. No?

You sure about that?

YOSSARIAT. Buddy?

BUDDY. Boo!

The TEXAN *jumps back. They laugh, except* YOSSARIAT.
BUDDY *backs off. The* TEXAN *scowls after him.* YOSSARIAT
goes to sit near the TEXAN.

YOSSARIAT. I'm sorry.

I want to apologise unreservedly for shouting at you earlier.

It's been such a terrible day.

TEXAN. Thank you.

I accept your apology.

Unreservedly also.

He laughs.

It has been a helluva day, hasn't it?

YOSSARIAT. Yes, it has.

TEXAN. There were times back there I think even Red Adair
would've shook his head and said:

'Too hot for me.'

YOSSARIAT. I'm sorry?

TEXAN. Red Adair. He's a firefighter. Used to do all the big rig
fires, oil fires.

That's my field.

Oil.

Discovery and procurement of.

I'm semi-retired now, of course. But in my day.

Pendleton the Gusher-King.

That's what they called me.

I could find oil in a stone in the desert.

YOSSARIAT. Oh fuck. You've got the wrong sand-niggers. There's no oil here.

TEXAN. Not yet maybe.

YOSSARIAT. Not never.

TEXAN. Oh, you can never say never.

YOSSARIAT *looks at him curiously, then dismisses him. He closes his eyes. For a moment the cannabis makes him feel almost human. Peace. But the* TEXAN *has a story to tell.*

I mean sure. Historically. Israel ain't exactly known for its oil.

But say a friend of your government's.

A pious man.

Say this pious man who prayed night and day for Israel's safety should some night awake from a dream.

And say he should remember that in that dream the hand of God had led him by Galilee.

And the voice of God had whispered in his ear.

And say as God's breath touched the pious man's ear the sky had blistered into brillant gold fire and a vision projected across the land, and all saw.

Pitch black crude. Bubbling fiery gold.

And say what God's voice had whispered were co-ordinates.

And say the pious man he wrote them down.

And say when he checked a map they pinpointed a spot in the Dead Sea.

In Israeli waters.

And say initial surveys showed significant encouragement to drill right there, where God said.

Say all that happened and all that was true.

Wouldn't that be something?

His question lies in the air, awaiting a response. It strikes YOSSARIAT *that the* TEXAN *may be sincere. He opens his eyes to see the* TEXAN*'s face.* YOSSARIAT *is tickled pink.*

YOSSARIAT. What?

Is that what you're doing here?

Looking for oil?

TEXAN. Well, I can't really talk about that.

YOSSARIAT. Oh, go on!

Buddy!

He's discovered oil.

Joe Texas discovered oil.

We're rich.

BUDDY. Is he sane?

YOSSARIAT. I don't know.

He said God told him the co-ordinates, if that helps any?

They both collapse laughing. The TEXAN*'s face goes red.*

TEXAN. You'll be laughing on the other side of your face
someday.

I have a lifetime's experience in this.

The oil is definitely there.

YOSSARIAT. Tell us another one.

TEXAN. It's a big deal, son.

Bigger than any you'll ever make.

It'll transform this country.

You'll see.

We're talking about oil here.

Oil.

And oil.

Will.

Set. You.

Free.

YOSSARIAT *looks at the* TEXAN, *remembering the last time
such promises were made.*

YOSSARIAT. They used to say that about work.

They were wrong.

The RABBI'S WIFE *shivers in her sleep.* BUDDY *looks in on her.*

BUDDY. So what's your cut, Tex?

TEXAN. What?

BUDDY. Your cut?

You know?

Moo-lah?

He makes the international sign for money.

TEXAN. Not a cent.

I'm not asking one penny.

YOSSARIAT. The goodness of your heart?

The TEXAN *makes a grand gesture. The sap is rising in amongst all this testosterone.*

TEXAN. It's my gift to your country, son.

To make your country strong.

BUDDY. My country is strong.

TEXAN. Not really, son.

There's an awful lot of stuff propping you up.

BUDDY. Do you see anything propping me up? Do you?

TEXAN. Son, all I'm looking at right now is an American gun.

And I'm guessing that inside it there are American bullets.

So maybe the guy holding it's speaking Russian or Armenian or Hebrew or whatever.

But it's the gun where the strength is. Not the man.

BUDDY *drops his hands and walks away. He snarls back.*

BUDDY. A gun's no use without the will to shoot it.

TEXAN. You can have all the will in the world, son.

Without the bullets, nobody's doing any dying.

YOSSARIAT *has had enough of this shit.*

YOSSARIAT. We don't need your guns.

We've taken on vast armies before and defeated them with a sling shot.

We'll do the same again.

TEXAN. That was a long time ago, son.

And that wasn't you.

YOSSARIAT. So this exercises you, does it? Israel's strength?

TEXAN. Son, Israel has to be strong.

BUDDY. Why?

Forgive my bluntness.

I'm curious.

TEXAN. Son, Israel has to be strong because Israel's the key to opening up the future.

Didn't you know that?

YOSSARIAT. What future?

BUDDY *finds that amusing. The* TEXAN *doesn't. He works on* BUDDY, *a more susceptible soul to conversion.*

TEXAN. The written future, son. God's time.

YOSSARIAT *laughs. The* TEXAN *ignores him.*

BUDDY. What the fuck is he talking about?

YOSSARIAT. The end of the world.

BUDDY *is disorientated. The* TEXAN *moves in for the kill.*

TEXAN. Don't tell me you don't feel it?

Don't tell me you don't think we're living through the final days?

This world is accelerating out of control, son.

A hundred years ago if you wanted to get somewhere fast you jumped on a horse.

Nowadays even space travel's passé.

However many hundreds of thousands or millions of miles away that moon is, the fact that men have walked there fills no child with awe.

Fifteen years ago no one had ever even heard of the internet, now it's there, in every home, spewing out its filth and poison. Corrupting everyone who comes into contact with it.

Hell, everywhere you look there's a war.

A few years ago the sea rose up and swallowed – just swallowed – however many hundreds of thousand souls. You ever heard of that before?

This world is jumping up and down like a jack-in-the-box, spiralling out of control, just jumping and jumping and spewing and laughing with this crazy insane painted idiot drooling clown mask face just jumping and lolling, jumping and lolling.

Everywhere I look all I see is that face.

This world is never going to be pushed back into its box again.

The lid is never going to be closed.

Tell me, soldier, tell me you don't feel it.

Tell me we are not living through the last days?

BUDDY *can't. He wants to but he can't.*

So how long we got, hoss?

How long before little baby Jesus comes marching unto war?

You won't make me look a fool on this, son. You're the fool if you don't believe.

All the signs are there.

All the signs.

1948 – the creation of a Jewish state.

1967 – that miraculous, miraculous war.

You all thought you were dead, didn't you?

All those armies. Every border. Just ready to swamp you?

Six days it took to smote all those hordes and wrest back the biblical places.

Oh glory be, my heart just swells to think of those brave volunteers.

He clasps his hands and gazes towards heaven. Disappointment poisons his rapture.

But you never took the temple.

You were supposed to take the temple.

BUDDY. Temple Mount?

TEXAN. You coulda had it.

BUDDY. We do have it.

TEXAN. Yes, son, with a mosque on the top.

Your nation's holiest site has a mosque built on top of it.

Doesn't that make you mad?

Doesn't that make you doubt whatever it is you're fighting for?

BUDDY *blinks with incomprehension.*

BUDDY. Of course there's a mosque on top.

As long as there's a mosque on top we're still alive.

The minute something happens to that mosque we've got every Mohammedan scumbag from Saudi to Indonesia buying themselves rocket-launchers and getting on the first plane for the Lebanon. We got the Third World fucking War.

TEXAN. They wouldn't attack you, son.

Not with your firepower.

Hell, you're the biggest beast in the jungle, son.

You can do anything you please.

BUDDY. Can I?

TEXAN. You know you can.

BUDDY. What about this?

He takes the TEXAN*'s hat and puts it on.*

Can I do this?

How about this?

BUDDY *cuffs the* TEXAN*'s shoulder. The* TEXAN *looks concerned.*

Or this?

Or this?

Or this?

Each question is accompanied by increased force. YOSSARIAT
opens his eyes.

YOSSARIAT. Buddy.

He's in my care.

BUDDY *looks with contempt at the* TEXAN *as he backs off.*

BUDDY. Take a break.

SLOMO *comes away from the window.* BUDDY *takes his place.*
SLOMO *grabs up the porn magazine and finds a seat. The*
TEXAN *looks at* BUDDY, *but addresses* YOSSARIAT.

TEXAN. What's his problem?

YOSSARIAT. I don't know, hoss.

My guess is you.

You're a bit insensitive, you know?

TEXAN. Me?

YOSSARIAT. Mmmnh.

You've got a tendency to talk without really considering how
your words might appear to the person hearing them.

You're not entirely sensitive to their needs.

Thus? Insensitive.

TEXAN. Well, I'm sorry.

I apologise for that.

It was not my intention to offend.

YOSSARIAT. Buddy?

Joe Texas says he's sorry.

And we're sorry too, aren't we, Buddy?

You've just got to realise what a sensitive issue that mosque is to
us.

We're surrounded by tens of millions of underemployed young
men who'd like nothing better than a really overpowering
excuse to push us back into the sea.

And that mosque? If anything happened to that mosque . . . ?

I know why it bothers you.

You need that temple built so that Jesus can come.

It's the East Gate, isn't it, he's due to enter?

It's written, isn't it?

And if it's written it has to be true.

So now you're like a kid at Christmas who's suddenly realised he's living in a house without a chimney.

How's Santa Claus going to come if there's no chimney for him to come down?

Well, Santa Claus? That's your mum and dad. And Jesus?

He's not coming.

He won't even phone.

TEXAN. You're a sorry excuse for a man.

YOSSARIAT. Am I not?

Well, maybe that's because I know what men are.

Maybe I don't want to be one any more.

The RABBI'S WIFE *appears in the doorway.*

RABBI'S WIFE. Buddy?

Do you have a light?

YOSSARIAT. And so my day is complete.

The RABBI'S WIFE *goes to* BUDDY *who lights her cigarette. She snuggles into his arm.*

RABBI'S WIFE. I'm cold.

I woke up and I didn't know where I was.

And I'm cold.

YOSSARIAT *rouses himself.*

YOSSARIAT. Oh, I'm fucking sorry!

It's hot enough out there if you fancy it.

Go on.

It's your country.

Walk your own streets.

See how far you get.

By this time tomorrow Al Jazeera will have sent your pictures around the world, strung up to a lamp post, your skirts flailing, your holy of holies pointing towards Mecca, a big sharp dildo stuffed up your crack.

RABBI'S WIFE. What is wrong with you?

YOSSARIAT. What's wrong with me?

What the fuck is wrong with you?

BUDDY. Chill, Yossariat.

RABBI'S WIFE. Yes, Yossariat. Chill.

She retrieves the whisky.

I bet you had a dog when you were a boy. Didn't you?

It was called Yossariat. Wasn't it?

And you'd be out in the backyard with it all the time –

Yossariat – Sit.

Yossariat – Stay.

Yossariat – Roll over.

I bet you did.

Interesting thing about dogs.

They instantly know who the leader is.

The top dog.

They don't have the same confusion as humans.

She picks up an imaginary stick and feigns throwing it.

Fetch.

Go on – fetch it, fetch. Yossariat.

Fetch.

YOSSARIAT *gives up. She smiles to* BUDDY.

I bet you did.

BUDDY. I shot a dog today.

RABBI'S WIFE. Did you?

BUDDY *nods.*

BUDDY. Yeah.

It was eating a greaseball kid.

The RABBI'S WIFE *laughs as she drinks, trying not to choke. She looks at* BUDDY.

RABBI'S WIFE. And you shot it?

For that?

A dog's got to eat.

BUDDY. Nobody's disputing a dog's right to eat.

The RABBI'S WIFE *strokes* BUDDY*'s chest and belly.*

RABBI'S WIFE. I like you, Buddy.

You like me, don't you?

Don't you?

BUDDY *puts an arm around her. She snuggles in. The* RABBI'S WIFE *notices* SLOMO *looking at her.*

Why is that boy staring at me?

In truth SLOMO*'s eyes have never left her since she walked in.*

BUDDY. Slomo?

RABBI'S WIFE. I don't know his name.

BUDDY. He's thinking about coming on your tits.

The RABBI'S WIFE *freezes for a second. As does* YOSSARIAT. *The game has somehow changed.*

RABBI'S WIFE. Oh Buddy, you're so funny.

BUDDY. No, seriously.

I know him.

I know every thought that's going through his head.

And right now that's what he's thinking about.

Spunking all over your tits.

She looks at SLOMO *again.*

RABBI'S WIFE. No?

BUDDY. Oh yeah.

RABBI'S WIFE. And what about you? What are you thinking about?

BUDDY. I'm thinking I should give my mum a ring.

It's been a while.

RABBI'S WIFE. Oh Buddy.

You're a bad man. You know that?

A bad, bad man.

Is that right, soldier?

She gets up and approaches SLOMO.

Is that what you're thinking about?

She puts her hands on her breasts and rubs, her eyes drilling into SLOMO.

Coming on my tits.

SLOMO *gets a bit bothered, dropping his magazine.*

What's that you're reading?

She grabs up the magazine. She looks at it and laughs.

My husband used to love me to do that to him.

Her laugh turns melancholy as she looks at the picture. Her gaze becomes sad. Her eyes don't leave the picture. BUDDY *comes to get her.*

BUDDY. Come on, Princess.

RABBI'S WIFE. It's true. He loved that. For me to take his – his glans – in my mouth.

Move my tongue lightly over it.

Hold it tight in my mouth.

My saliva.

Burned, he said.

My finger . . .

She puts her finger in her mouth and kisses it.

He liked me to put my finger up his ass.

Funny.

The TEXAN *is disappointed in the* RABBI'S WIFE.

TEXAN. You're really quite irreverent for a Rabbi's wife, aren't you?

She rounds on him with a glint of her old passion.

RABBI'S WIFE. You're stupid.

You stupid man.

That was reverence.

I was talking with reverence.

She looks around the room.

What?

He liked me to spread my legs for him?

What's wrong with that?

He was a man.

I was his wife.

You look at me as if I'm insane because I enjoyed my husband's cock inside me.

What's more normal than that?

I loved his cock inside me.

I loved him.

I loved him.

TEXAN. My dear . . .

RABBI'S WIFE. Get away from me.

TEXAN. I think she's had too much to drink.

RABBI'S WIFE. Did I ask you what you think? Did I?

Do you think I will ever care what you think again?

TEXAN. Now Rachel . . .

RABBI'S WIFE. He knows my name.

TEXAN. Of course I know your name. I was a great admirer of your husband. A friend, I think.

RABBI'S WIFE. Oh, you were his friend all right.

You know this man . . .

This man belongs to a church in America that has a congregation of ten thousand people.

Ten thousand, and not one leaves less than ten dollars in the collection plate every week.

Of course you were his friend.

Every day we thanked you.

And now I have the chance to thank you in person.

Well, thank you, Mr Texas.

Thank you for my Hermès scarves, my Louis Vuitton bags.

Thank you for the Cadillac.

TEXAN. That money was for . . .

RABBI'S WIFE. I know what the money was for.

Well, forget it. It's over,.

He's dead.

The state of Israel sent a message to me and my family.

It told us we were not wanted.

That even our existence was a threat.

There's no room for true believers in this world any more.

Unless you're the president of the United States.

And you're not. Are you, temple builder?

Because if you were the president you would have known.

If the Israeli army are going to gun down a dissident on a New York street corner then the president of the United States would have known.

TEXAN. I'm sorry.

RABBI'S WIFE. It's too late to apologise. Forget it. It's over.

He's dead.

He's dead and you're alive.

And he's alive. And he's alive.

And that's the world I live in now.

Without him.

With you.

And you.

And you.

Buddy. I'm cold. Will you put your arm around me?

BUDDY *puts his arm around her. She pushes him away and grabs her discarded bag. She blows her nose, being a brave girl again. Her weakness makes her angry with herself.*

BUDDY. What was the money for?

She shrugs.

RABBI'S WIFE. The temple.

Rebuilding the temple.

Why else would a Christian give money to a Jew?

Oh, the temple builder.

He wants to rebuild the temple, don't you, temple builder?

What it is with these Christians?

Their little Jesus can't come back without us – the Jews – rebuilding our shabby old temple for them.

Isn't that right, temple builder?

He's waiting, you know . . . Jesus . . . Up there.

Waiting to come back.

But he can't. Can he?

Because the stupid, lazy Jews haven't rebuilt their temple yet.

Isn't that right?

BUDDY. What about the mosque?

RABBI'S WIFE. What mosque?

BUDDY. Al-Aqsa?

The Dome of the Rock?

RABBI'S WIFE. Oh Buddy.

You see, hoss, back in Texas.

If we got niggers in.

Our woodpile.

We smoke 'em out, boy.

Just smoke 'em out.

And hell, if the smoke don't work, there's always dynamite.

TEXAN. What are you saying?

The RABBI'S WIFE *laughs.*

BUDDY. Is that true?

RABBI'S WIFE. Hey, if you've got rubbish in your garden, you just clear it out.

Don't you? Temple builder?

Just clear it out. Isn't that right?

Oh God, look at Yossariat. Has his mind finally gone?

YOSSARIAT *is crouched down beneath the window, hands clasped tightly between his knees.*

BUDDY. You should never underestimate the captain.

RABBI'S WIFE. Why's that?

BUDDY. You should just never underestimate him.

It's a bad thing to do.

RABBI'S WIFE. Oh Buddy? You're funny.

YOSSARIAT. Is that true?

TEXAN. Is what true?

YOSSARIAT. You were funding her husband?

You were giving them money to blow up the mosque?

TEXAN. No!

RABBI'S WIFE. Of course it's true. Look at him.

Even at breakfast he comes to me.

'Lady, I knew your husband. We had business. We did business.

Can I talk to you? Our business was unfinished. We need a new leader.

A strong leader. Someone that people will follow.'

TEXAN. Captain.

That woman is crazy.

I met her husband twice. I met her once.

We fund charitable projects all over.

RABBI'S WIFE. And of course there was money. Always money.

Buddy?

You know what we did one day?

Money. A bag. We spread it on the bed.

Naked. A gold bar to masturbate with.

Buddy. My back was green with it.

Like grass strains.

Greenbacks. We had greenbacks.

TEXAN. My Lord.

I regret the day I ever laid eyes on you.

And your pervert husband.

YOSSARIAT. Bastard!

YOSSARIAT *punches his stomach. The* TEXAN *goes down quick and clean.*

You fucking bastard! Tell me.

Is it true?

RABBI'S WIFE. Of course it's true. I'm telling you.

YOSSARIAT. I want to hear it!

I want to hear it from his own mouth!

The TEXAN *gets up, holding his stomach.*

TEXAN. This woman is a liar!

BUDDY *stops the* TEXAN's *lunge at the laughing* RABBI'S WIFE.

YOSSARIAT. You never paid them?

You never paid them to attack the mosque?

TEXAN. No.

RABBI'S WIFE. My husband says, 'The temple waits for God.'

Tex Ritter says, 'Sometimes God needs a little push.'

TEXAN. No.

RABBI'S WIFE. My husband says, 'This is too much. How many will die?'

Donald Rumsfeld says, 'Hell, son, you can't make an omelette without cracking eggs.'

TEXAN. Why are you doing this to me?

You know it's not true.

RABBI'S WIFE. My husband says, 'What the fuck you doing taking cooking lessons off Donald Rumsfeld?' Tex Ritter says, 'He da man.'

'He da man!'

TEXAN. Captain? You gotta believe me.

The only time I've ever talked about the temple is in the context of the future.

I never advocated.

I never advocated.

The TEXAN *shakes his head.*

We're Christians for God's sake.

Americans.

Doesn't that mean anything still?

The RABBI'S WIFE *is in* YOSSARIAT*'s ear.*

RABBI'S WIFE. Look at him. Mr Squeaky-Clean-Butter-Wouldn't-Melt.

Listen to what he says out loud.

But his fevered dreams say –

'My lifetime, Lord, my lifetime.

Make it happen in my lifetime or I will.

I, thy blasphemer.

With my dirty feet in your temple.

I, Joe Texas, will make it happen still.'

TEXAN. We funded them. To build the temple. Not destroy the mosque!

RABBI'S WIFE. Is there a difference?

YOSSARIAT. Oh, you fucking bitch!

YOSSARIAT *attacks the* TEXAN, *a flurry of blows more akin to an upset child than the ruthless efficiency of a Special Forces soldier.*

73

What kind of fucking man are you, to wish such a thing on the world.

Tell me, you bitch!

What kind of a fucking bitch are you?

The TEXAN *rises from the ground with a bloody face and the intensity of a demon, pinning* YOSSARIAT *against the wall. He drops him. He wipes his mouth and spits.*

TEXAN. Son, there is nothing I would not do for the Glory of Jesus Christ!

BUDDY. Yossariat!

A rocket-propelled grenade hits the outside of the building. A huge explosion rocks the walls and the ceiling. The men run for their guns. SLOMO *gets to the window first, emptying his magazine out onto the street.* BUDDY *throws his back against the wall beside the window. When* SLOMO *hits the ground he jumps into the window and sprays the street.* YOSSARIAT *leaves the* TEXAN *to find a space at the window, but doesn't shoot. He turns inside.*

YOSSARIAT. Stop it. Stop it. We're shooting at ghosts.

We're shooting at ghosts.

YOSSARIAT *falls to his knees. The* TEXAN *laughs.*

The TEXAN *and the* RABBI'S WIFE *look at each other. There is sadness and hurt in their eyes, and betrayal in the air between them. The* RABBI'S WIFE *laughs and raises the bottle.*

RABBI'S WIFE. Cheers.

She laughs.

Lights.

FIVE

Later. The TEXAN *dozes – he has his hat back. The* RABBI'S WIFE *is also sleeping, either in the room or in the other room, depending on the tastes of the production.* YOSSARIAT *and* BUDDY *are sitting against a wall, sharing a joint. They're more relaxed, and a little giggly to begin with – a stifled gigglyness.*

YOSSARIAT. Well, it's been a strange little day, hasn't it?

BUDDY. You should've been here yesterday.

YOSSARIAT. Why? What happened?

No, don't tell me.

I don't know if I'm dehumanised enough to hear the grisly details.

BUDDY. Don't underestimate yourself.

There's a limit to human evil.

YOSSARIAT. No. There's nothing new under the sun.

Look at him. Pig. Like butter wouldn't melt.

How can he sleep and I can't?

BUDDY. He's old.

YOSSARIAT. He would destabilise a country, an entire region, just to fulfil some sick, stupid.

Fantasy. What kind of people are they? These Americans?

BUDDY. Fuck them.

YOSSARIAT. Yeah. Fuck them. Fuck him. Fuck her.

Oh fuck.

I hope they do it, you know?

I hope they fucking pull it off.

Let them blow up the mosque, blow it to smithereens.

I hope they fuck off every Muslim in the entire fucking world, oh fuck no, let's not limit ourselves.

I hope they fuck off every human being on this entire planet.

I hope they send armies.

Vast armies.

I hope they provoke us to the worst atrocities this planet has ever seen.

I hope the fucking Pakistanis get involved. Go nuclear.

Yeah, go on, you fuckers, make us take out the big guns.

We'll see what they've got then.

If they want Armageddon they can fucking have it.

I hate this fucking world.

BUDDY. What's the deal with the temple anyway? My parents never came here for a fucking temple. They came here for fresh oranges and colour TV.

YOSSARIAT. MTV and internet porn.

BUDDY. Why not? Beats shit out of this.

YOSSARIAT *shakes his head.*

YOSSARIAT. No. Messianic fervour is the lifeblood of the universe.

You can live without it. But you can't be alive.

You're living, see, but it's all a bit flat. A bit lifeless.

You need a cause. It's part of the condition.

My mother told me that.

When I was four.

When I was five.

When I was six.

When I was seven.

Fuck it.

I don't want to go back there I think.

There's nothing to go back for.

She's put an end to all that.

Shit job anyway.

Advertising.

It's funny.

Not what I wanted for myself.

I meant to study French literature.

Romantic drama.

De Rostand.

You know *Cyranno*?

The nose?

He jumps up onto a piece of furniture, imaginary sword raised and salutes the dead young men of Gascony.

'These were the Gascony Cadets!'

The TEXAN *moves in his sleep.* YOSSARIAT *feels ridiculous.*

Fuck it.

I'll maybe stay here.

Never go back.

Flit from house to house.

Live off rats.

Live on the streets like a dog.

A rat-eating dog.

On the frontier between the earth and heaven.

I'll walk these desert streets. Until the Messiah comes.

Or my bones return to the desert.

Hosanna.

BUDDY. The Messiah isn't coming, mate.

YOSSARIAT. I know.

He won't even. Phone.

Still.

BUDDY. I tell you.

Getting out of Odessa was a big enough cause for my people.

Every day you wake up and there's milk to drink for breakfast.

Bless those days.

They miss Odessa though.

I miss Odessa and I've never been.

The air's not right here.

All my family find it hard to breathe.

BUDDY *sees* SLOMO *yawning.*

Take a break, man.

You've been standing there all day.

YOSSARIAT. The lone sentinel.

Keeping back the Caliphate.

BUDDY *caresses* SLOMO*'s back as he moves inside.*
YOSSARIAT *hands him something to eat.*

You've done well today.

I'm proud of you.

The praise makes SLOMO *happy. He cheekily asks:*

SLOMO. Will I get a medal?

YOSSARIAT. You want a medal?

Here.

Take mine.

YOSSARIAT *goes in his pocket and takes out a medal. It is
quite beautiful and obviously means something.* SLOMO *takes it
and looks at it. He is struck by the beauty. His mouth is open, as
is his habit when thinking.* BUDDY *nods.*

BUDDY. Nice.

SLOMO. Is that the one you got for Belmina?

SLOMO *looks at* YOSSARIAT. YOSSARIAT *looks back
smiling, saying nothing.*

I don't want that.

SLOMO *presses it back into* YOSSARIAT*'s hand.*

YOSSARIAT. No.

It's not worth much.

Is it?

YOSSARIAT *drops the medal on the floor. The* TEXAN *snorts
in his sleep.* YOSSARIAT *turns back to* SLOMO, *who is
stretching to look at the* RABBI'S WIFE.

BUDDY. You were there too?

YOSSARIAT *shrugs.*

YOSSARIAT. I'm not proud.

The weight of the world crushes YOSSARIAT. *As he passes*
SLOMO *he says in a weak voice:*

You can fuck her now.

If you want.

SLOMO. Seriously?

He looks to BUDDY. BUDDY *is just staring. He looks to*
YOSSARIAT.

YOSSARIAT. It's okay.

SLOMO *goes to the* RABBI'S WIFE.

BUDDY. Yossariat?

YOSSARIAT. Forget it.

It's just the war.

YOSSARIAT *and* BUDDY *sink down the wall and sit and
watch as* SLOMO *gently pulls down the* RABBI'S WIFE*'s
underwear. She moves in her stupor.* SLOMO *puts his hand over
her mouth then prepares to rape her. She wakes up, fear slowly
overtaking her, a slight sound coming from beneath* SLOMO*'s
hand.*

BUDDY. You're worse than they are.

YOSSARIAT *nods.*

YOSSARIAT. I know.

I'm not entirely sane.

They watch as the RABBI'S WIFE *struggles. She gets her
mouth free and screams, fighting back. The* TEXAN *jumps
awake. He hears the rumpus, looks at the soldiers, realises
they're not going to help, and leaps to the* RABBI'S WIFE*'s aid.
He pulls* SLOMO *off her and throws him across the room.*
SLOMO *and the* TEXAN *fight.* YOSSARIAT *and* BUDDY *get
to their feet. The* RABBI'S WIFE *is shouting:*

RABBI'S WIFE. Help me. Help me. He was raping me. He . . .
He . . . Help me.

BUDDY *comforts her.* YOSSARIAT *takes something heavy and
cracks it down on the* TEXAN*'s shoulders/head, knocking him
out.*

Oh my God. Oh my God. He raped me. He raped me.

Don't you hear me?

He raped me.

That man raped me.

You are a witness.

And you are a . . .

She throws herself at SLOMO, *raining down blows which he shields himself from like a child.*

You bastard!

You raped me!

You will be castrated for this.

You will be cas. Trated.

There is a gunshot. SLOMO *jumps aside. The* RABBI'S WIFE *falls.* BUDDY *is holding* YOSSARIAT's *pistol. The* RABBI'S WIFE *flails about on the floor. She roars like an animal. And continues roaring until she dies. They watch her until she dies.*

SLOMO. You. You. Killed her.

BUDDY. Yeah. Rat-a-tat-tat.

Whatever YOSSARIAT *was expecting, he looks stunned by what's taken place.*

Can you get me a drink? Please.

YOSSARIAT. Yeah, course.

YOSSARIAT *picks up the bottle and hands it to* BUDDY. BUDDY *bends at the knees over the* RABBI'S WIFE. *He takes a drink.*

SLOMO. Did I do that?

YOSSARIAT *shakes his head. He puts his hand around* SLOMO's *neck and leads him away.*

Lights.

SIX

They have strung the TEXAN *up on the wall in a parody of Christ. They have gagged him and put a black hood over his head. Then they have put his cowboy hat back on.* YOSSARIAT *looks at the* TEXAN, *then comes back to sit with* BUDDY, *who is drinking.* SLOMO *is at the window.*

YOSSARIAT. Buddy. You truly are an artist.

BUDDY. Put a record on, eh? He probably likes all that cowboy shit.

YOSSARIAT. Slomo. Put a record on.

SLOMO. Which one?

YOSSARIAT. Any one. Any one with a cowboy on the cover.

SLOMO *goes through the records and takes one out.*

You want to see his dick?

BUDDY *giggles.* YOSSARIAT *stands close to the* TEXAN. *The* TEXAN *bellows and struggles against his bonds.*

What is it with Americans and homosexuality? They're worse than the greaseballs.

As if me putting my hands on his balls would make him any less a man.

I've got half a mind to wank him off just to destroy his ego.

The TEXAN *bellows again.*

My, but you're feisty.

Hey, maybe I'll cook it up so he's got his dick in the merry widow's mouth.

Take a photo. Post it on the internet.

Every time somebody punches in a Google search, up it comes.

How about that?

You like that?

The TEXAN *struggles.*

Never had sex with a dead person before?

YOSSARIAT *turns away to join* BUDDY.

Everybody knows these Christians are depraved.

BUDDY. They're not the only ones.

The music comes on. It's 'If You Don't Like Hank Williams (You Can Kiss My Ass)' by Kris Kristofferson.

YOSSARIAT. Oh, I like this. You like this, Tex?

You fuck!

SLOMO *comes across to* BUDDY *and sits.*

SLOMO. Like the guy.

Guy said he was God.

BUDDY. Yeah. It's a parody.

He looks up towards YOSSARIAT *who is standing looking up at the* TEXAN, *drinking.*

We'd better get going, eh? People will be wondering where we are.

BUDDY *gets up to collect their stuff.*

SLOMO. Why's the captain mad at George-Bush?

BUDDY. I don't know. George-Bush believes things. The captain doesn't.

SLOMO. What does he believe?

BUDDY. Well, you know the guy thought he was God. George-Bush believes he really was God. He thinks that after they killed him, he lay in his grave for three days. Then he crawled out. And someday he's going to come back again. And make everything better again.

SLOMO. Is he?

BUDDY *smiles and pats* SLOMO*'s back.* YOSSARIAT *pulls off the* TEXAN*'s hood. He throws his hat to* SLOMO, *who catches it, delighted.*

BUDDY. Heading back, captain.

You okay for cleaning up?

YOSSARIAT. Yeah.

YOSSARIAT *has a can of paraffin in his hand. He splashes some around the floor.*

BUDDY. See you later, Tex.

BUDDY *pats the* TEXAN*'s stomach. His eyes widen.* YOSSARIAT *douses him in petrol. He struggles.*

SLOMO *has gone to the window to get his magazine. He looks out for one last time.*

SLOMO. Whole world's on fire.

BUDDY *raises his hand in a half-arsed clenched-fist salute.*

BUDDY. Shalom.

> YOSSARIAT's *salute is even more feeble. He mouths the word rather than say it. His hand hangs in the air.*

Come on, cowboy. Let's go home.

> BUDDY *and* SLOMO *leave.* YOSSARIAT *continues with the tidy-up, dragging the* RABBI'S WIFE's *body through and dousing it as the* TEXAN *struggles. The record needle comes to the end and goes back to the start. Reprise: 'If You Don't Like Hank Williams'.* YOSSARIAT *sits, exhausted. He repeats the clenched-fist salute, his hand taking on a life of its own, beating* YOSSARIAT's *chest and shoulders as he stares at something so sad and vile he can't name it.* YOSSARIAT *shows emotion. Any emotion will do.*

A Nick Hern Book

Petrol Jesus Nightmare #5 first published in Great Britain in 2006 as a paperback original by Nick Hern Books Limited, 14 Larden Road, London W3 7ST, in association with the Traverse Theatre, Edinburgh

Cover image: Anna Crolla, featuring Joseph Thompson as Yossariat

Typeset by Country Setting, Kingsdown, Kent CT14 8ES
Printed and bound in Great Britain by Bookmarque, Croydon, Surrey

A CIP catalogue record for this book is available from the British Library

ISBN-10   1 85459 953 4
ISBN-13   978 1 85459 953 7